Franciscans and the Scriptures

Living in the Word of God

Washington Theological Union
Symposium Papers
2005

Franciscans and the Scriptures

Living in the Word of God

Washington Theological Union Symposium Papers 2005

Edited by

Elise Saggau, O.S.F.

The Franciscan Institute
St. Bonaventure University
St. Bonaventure, New York

CFIT/ESC-OFM Series
Number 5

The articles in this book were originally presented
at a symposium sponsored by the Franciscan Center
at Washington Theological Union, Washington, DC,
May 27-29, 2005.
This publication is the fifth in a series of documents
resulting from the work of the
Commission on the Franciscan Intellectual Tradition of the
English-speaking Conference of the
Order of Friars Minor
(CFIT/ESC-OFM).

Cover design: Jennifer L. Davis

ISBN: 157659-1387

Library of Congress Control Number
2006921230

Printed and bound in the United States of America

BookMasters, Inc.
Ashland, Ohio

TABLE OF CONTENTS

PREFACE

For those of us who are Christian, the Word of God is a primary experience of the Divine. It is more than a mere carrier of ideas framed in concise propositions. It is, as much Scriptural scholarship maintains today, a life-changing, transformative encounter with the Father, Christ the Anointed One and the life-giving Spirit. It is an invitation into the life of the Spirit and an affirmation of each person's human destiny. This awareness is the gift of the last sixty years in Roman Catholic biblical scholarship, a scholarship that continues to nourish the Christian faithful and to develop and deepen our faith.

It was not always so. When I first studied Scripture in the late 1950s, it was a dismal experience indeed. Texts were used to prove a point of doctrine without careful examination of the texts' exegetical or critical meaning. We need to remember, however, in the late '50s it had been only sixteen years since Pius XII had penned *Divino Afflante Spiritus* (1943), the *Magna Carta* of contemporary Roman Catholic scripture scholarship. It authorized employing form criticism as a tool for exegesis and encouraged serious study of biblical and especially Semitic languages. Unfortunately, that liberating document had not filtered down to many Catholic seminaries and schools of theology—and so students found themselves studying material that had questionable scholarly provenance. Such is not the case anymore, evidenced by this present volume and its exploration of the Franciscan tradition and biblical scholarship.

Today, Roman Catholic biblical scholarship is robust, scholarly and pastoral, due to the second foundational document of Catholic biblical studies. Vatican Council II's constitution *Dei Verbum* occasioned a flood of respectable Catholic scholarship in the years that followed. This scholarship is gradually transforming Roman Catholicism into an evangelized and evangelizing community that enthusiastically recognizes the Scriptures as the *norma non normanda*, nourishing and guiding all Christian discipleship.

This present volume by four noted Franciscan scholars evidences that strength in its range and depth. Each author takes a different path into Franciscan history and biblical study. For example, Robert Karris, O.F.M., Th.D., a member of the research faculty of the Franciscan Institute at St. Bonavenutre University, and a prolific author in New Testament studies, offers a penetrating and thoroughly enriching study of the relationship of Bonaventure's Christology to that of the Gospel of Luke. His particular emphases are varied and rich, steeped especially in the warmth and insight of Bonaventure's spiritual and scholarly thought. Particularly significant are the numerous insights Karris has into Bonaventure's way of spiritual interpretation in handling the Scriptures and how he drew keenly practical spiritual guidance from them.

An engaging study of the Gospel of John and the life of Francis of Assisi by James Scullion, O.F.M., Ph.D., Assistant Professor at WTU, enunciates in a different voice the meaning of a spiritual reading of Scripture. Scullion cleverly draws on the musical genius of John Coltrane, the well-known jazz saxophonist, using it as an analog for understanding the method of scriptural reading employed by Francis and many medieval mystics who prayed over and lived out the Gospel in their daily lives. Coltrane was able to penetrate the very depth of music and craft a new interpretation that both expanded the music and yet remained faithful to the text. Just so, says Scullion, the Gospel of John is embedded in many of the admonitions of Francis, who draws on Johannine titles for Jesus in much of his preaching and guidance of the brothers. If one can say that Francis interpreted a text, he did it much as Coltrane did—expanding the text through living it while remaining faithful to it in its verbal expression.

According to Scullion, Francis sees the Gospel as revelation, as mission and as promise. In this, Francis's reading is deeply ecclesial—it approaches the Word of God in depth and from this Word derives the motivation to go forth in mission to announce the promise it brings to the human family. For Francis, the Word of God is the primary text of all preaching and teaching. Of course we remember the aptness of a famous dictum often attributed to Francis: "Preach always; sometimes use words."

Dominic Monti, O.F.M., Ph.D., former professor at the Washington Theological Union and St. Bonaventure University, raises a key question for all of us who are students and disciples of the Franciscan tradition. He asks the simple but trenchant question: "Do the Scriptures make a difference in our lives?" This exploration of our response builds on the foundational role that the Scriptures played in the life of Francis. Admittedly, Francis lived in a different time and in a different world. Yet we Franciscans continue to claim we are an evangelical family. So the challenge is this: is there a genuine, integral Franciscan evangelical foundation to our lives?

Clearly, among contemporary evangelical Christians, the Bible is vibrantly alive and taken by many as a guide for living out the Christian faith. Is it possible to be Catholic *and* evangelical at the same time? The "Franciscan Movement" claims it is. Professor Monti explores that claim. He invites us to go beyond historical-critical methodology into the deeper realm of personal, life-long, and life-enhancing commitments to the Gospel. In doing so, he reflects in a scholarly fashion the old saying that it is not enough to talk the talk, we also need to walk the walk. Reading the Scriptures should be an encounter with God, an invitation to prayer that is open, trusting and transformative. Monti's analysis of word as symbol and Scripture as potentially revelatory, with a nod to Sandra Schneiders, provides a truly engaging essay.

Michael Guinan, O.F.M, Ph.D., esteemed long-term professor of Old Testament at the Franciscan School of Theology in Berkeley, brings his narrative talent to the task of opening up the riches of Wisdom literature and its role in the Franciscan tradition. He guides us to a deep appreciation of the role of wisdom in the writings of Francis. While few specific quotes from Wisdom literature appear in Francis's *oeuvre*, Francis is a person endowed with wisdom, evidenced by his esteem for creation—and not just nature. For him creation is a holy statement writ large in the skies, sea and earth. As such, it renders God intelligible to each and every created person. The beauty and meaning of the universe limns the loving creative power of God. The work of creation is God's house. If all creation is God's house and temple and we live, move and have our being in that house, then we are all sisters and brothers, regardless of the accidents of class, race, gender or economic status. We can see, then, why Francis could sing the beauty of creation in his *Canticle of the Creatures* and regard every human person as a fellow pilgrim on the way.

The contribution of careful biblical scholarship to the "Franciscan Movement" yields a rich harvest of insight and depth. First, it is immediately nourishing for those of us who are heirs and followers of Francis and Clare. Secondly, this approach lives right at the heart of Francis's genius in that he viewed the Word of God as an experience of real presence. His deep, life-changing devotion to the Word now becomes our deep, life-transforming experience. Thirdly, such study and scholarship as presented in this volume introduce our "Catholic evangelicalism" into an ecumenical relationship with mainline *and* Evangelical Protestantism, because we can now all be reading from the same page. This is a genuine ecumenical advance on a grass-roots level.

What of the future? If this is indeed a life-sustaining Word, then it necessarily looks to the future—and particularly for us Franciscans to the ongoing development and deepening of the Franciscan charism within the larger mantle of the Word of God in the Church. A question that frequently crosses my mind is whether we Franciscans can look to a Church that mirrors the deep values of Francis—a Church that is evangelical, Catholic and reformed. The genius of Francis was to lift the focus of his vision from the accepted cultural mores of the Middle Ages and reach back and beyond them to the New Testament and the testimony of Jesus. Yet, he did this not in a restorationist or antiquarian manner, but precisely in a way that made it liveable and relevant in his time and culture.

Yet, he also did this within the Catholic tradition and in close association with the Catholic Church. He was able to bridge the gap that had developed between the Church and the many popular approaches to being "poor disciples," who often became separated from the Church. By bridging that gap, and by remaining rooted in the Gospel, Francis articulated the foundations for reform in the Church. His life was evangelical, Catholic and reforming. I suggest that paradigm is still vital, but needs to be reinterpreted for our time and culture. This volume is a valuable step forward on that journey.

Vincent Cushing, O.F.M.
President Emeritus
Washington Theological Union
February, 2006

NOTE: Due to a variety of difficulties the lecture by Joseph Mindling, O.F.M. Cap. , "Pauline Themes in the Life and Writings of Francis," will be printed in another venue.

CHAPTER ONE

DO THE SCRIPTURES
MAKE A DIFFERENCE IN OUR LIVES?

Dominic V. Monti, O.F.M.

Since this is a gathering of Franciscans, it is only appropriate that we begin with a story. This one was first told by St. Bonaventure in a letter to a young master of arts who was considering becoming a friar:

> That you might appreciate how much the study of Holy Scripture delighted St. Francis, let me tell you what I myself heard from a brother who is still living. Once a New Testament came into Francis's hands, and since so many brothers could not use it all at once, he pulled the leaves apart and distributed the pages among them. Thus each one could read it and not be a hindrance to others.[1]

Today we are addressing a question: "Do the Scriptures make a difference in our lives?" This little story suggests that Francis would have thought the answer obvious. He probably would not have even thought of raising the question. For him, God's written words—even only a page!—offered a precious feast to be savored by every one of his brothers and sisters.

We contemporary Franciscans—at least in theory—continue to insist on the centrality of the Bible in our spiritual life. I would imagine that every Franciscan community has a passage in its legislation similar to this one from the General Constitutions of the Friars Minor:

> Since the life and Rule of the Friars Minor is to observe the Holy Gospel, the friars are to apply themselves to the reading of and meditation on the Holy Gospel and other Scriptures, so that understanding the Word of God, they may attain to the perfection of their state more fully.[2]

Actually, such sentiments would not have been expressed two or three generations ago. They reflect the remarkable biblical renaissance in the Catholic Church since the publication of Pius XII's encyclical *Di-*

vino afflante Spiritu in 1943 that bore fruit in the Constitution *Dei Verbum* of the Second Vatican Council. That document "forcefully and specifically" exhorted "those who lead the religious life to learn the surpassing knowledge of Jesus Christ by frequent reading of the divine Scriptures, for 'ignorance of the Scriptures is ignorance of Christ.'"[3] In contrast, pre-conciliar manuals of Franciscan spirituality hardly mentioned the role of the Bible. They based their idea of Franciscan spiritual life on observance of the Rule—considered as a legal document—and emphasized participation in the Eucharist and a commitment to traditional ascetical and devotional practices, especially mental prayer.

However, despite the theoretical place of Scripture in our Franciscan lives, the question we are posing is a very real one: what difference does Scripture *actually* make in our lives? Even though today we are blessed with a rich three-year cycle of biblical readings in the lectionary, excellent commentaries filled with the latest scholarship and a virtual explosion of homily preparation services, the Bible itself is often not central to our spiritual lives. So often, those of us who are ordained open our Bibles mainly when we are preparing talks to present to other people; indeed, the multiplicity of study aids can actually dispense us from the task of personally immersing ourselves in the Word of God. Others of us choose only the readings we like to hear. Like people who play their favorite CDs over and over again, we narrow God's revelation to what will re-enforce our prejudices rather than challenge us.

But perhaps our greatest problem, whether we approach the Bible as somewhat naïve fundamentalists or with the best techniques of the historical-critical method, arises from what remains essentially a one-dimensional approach to Scripture. I think most of us—particularly, perhaps, those of us who have received a formal theological training—almost reflexively approach the Bible simply as an object: a text "out there" that we examine. "What is the message?" "What's it saying to us?" These are the questions we immediately tend to ask. And such questions raise in turn a more utilitarian one: "What techniques should I use to unpack it?" In other words, how do I dissect this object to uncover its message?

I would like to suggest that such questions are not the first ones to pose if indeed we want the Scriptures "to make a difference in our lives." Here I find the approach of the great Protestant theologian Karl Barth to be instructive.[4] Barth was convinced that the historical-critical method that characterized modern biblical studies, although certainly helpful for interpreting the text, could not remain the exclusive, or even dominant approach, precisely because it viewed that text as an object to be dissected. It asks:

> What is there behind all these words (in the Bible) that labors for expression? This is a dangerous question. We might do better not to come too near this burning bush. For we are sure to betray what is—*behind* us! The Bible gives to every person and to every era such answers to their questions as they deserve. We shall always find in it as much as we seek and no more: high and divine content if it is high and divine content that we seek; transitory and "historical" content, if it is transitory and "historical" content that we seek; nothing whatever if it is nothing whatever that we seek. The hungry are satisfied by it, and to the satisfied it is surfeiting before they have even opened it. The question, What is within the Bible? has a mortifying way of converting itself into the opposing question, Well, what are you looking for, and who are you, pray, who make bold to look?[5]

In other words, Barth is suggesting that our usual question, "What's the text saying?" should be preceded by two others: "Who am *I*?" and "What *do* I seek?"

For Scripture to make a difference in our lives, these questions must be in the forefront. We must hear it and read it with the conviction that we are truly encountering God's Word *to us.* We must read the Scripture because we *want* to hear *God's* Word. For a believer, reading the Scripture has to be an act of prayer. Like all prayer, it must be sparked by a desire to enter into a relationship with God. Perhaps we have forgotten another mandate of the same decree that focused attention on the role of Scripture: "Let them remember that prayer should accompany the reading of Sacred Scripture, so that it becomes a dialogue between God and the human reader. 'For we speak to him when we pray; we listen to him when we read the divine oracles.'"[6] Like other forms of prayer, reading the Scripture must be an encounter between a seeker (a human listener) and a giver (the divine speaker), an encounter mediated in this case by written words, an encounter that calls the seeker to deeper life.

This was certainly the case for Francis. As a relatively uneducated layperson, Francis had a profound reverence for the written Word of God. It is interesting that he never speaks of "the Bible" or "Holy Scripture," in the sense of a book containing a collection of inspired writings. Rather, he speaks of "the Word of God," or of "the most holy words of the Lord," or "God's holy written words."[7] There is almost an iconic sense of the text here—these writings are not mere historical documents, but words that make Christ actively present.

Indeed, in Francis's mind, there is a strong parallel between the Eucharist and God's holy words precisely as sacraments. As Norbert Nguyen-Van-Khanh has pointed out: "In Francis's own writings we find this surprising fact: every time he speaks of the Body and Blood of Christ, he also speaks of his Holy Word."[8] Francis draws this parallel seven times. For example, in his *Exhortation to the Clergy,* Francis urges reverence for both the reserved Eucharist and the Scriptures, keeping them both in special places: "For we have and see nothing bodily of the Most High in this world except his Body and Blood, his names and words through which we have been made and redeemed from death to life." In fact, he even gives the Word a certain precedence: "We know it cannot be His Body without being first consecrated by the word [of the institution narrative]."[9] And in his *Testament* he uses the same word— "minister"—to speak of the work of the clergy with regard to both the Eucharist and God's Word:

> I see nothing corporally of the most high Son of God except his most holy Body and Blood which they [priests] receive and they alone minister to others. . . .And we must honor all theologians and those who minister the most holy divine words and respect them as those who minister to us spirit and life.[10]

Thus, like the liturgical sacraments, God's written words—however seemingly banal their content—are symbols that make present for us in a powerful way the reality they mediate.

A work that has contributed greatly to my own understanding of this fuller dimension of Scripture has been a book by Sandra Schneiders, *The Revelatory Text.* Here Schneiders has provided a lucid and compelling model of biblical interpretation, utilizing the insights of such thinkers as Paul Ricouer and Hans-Georg Gadamer, who have provided the theory behind much of contemporary hermeneutics. Schneiders emphasizes that the phrase "the Word of God" refers most basically to God's personal self-disclosure. Over the centuries, there has been a natural tendency to reduce the idea of revelation to a specific content—"the imparting of otherwise unavailable information." But we must remember that words by their very nature are not primarily objects in themselves, but the medium of our encounter with reality, especially other persons. We come to know each other by means of language. As persons move to a more intimate level, the dynamic of speaking and hearing is "not primarily the transfer of information but the mutual gift of selves."[11]

Words are not simply signs providing information, but symbols, "the mode of presence of something that cannot be encountered in any other way."[12] As Francis saw clearly, words are sacramental, bringing to expression an invisible presence. Words make an inner personal reality present and immediate.

To say that the Scriptures are the "Word of God" is actually to employ a metaphor; this phrase cannot be taken literally, because God is a pure spirit and cannot "speak." The reason Jews, Christians and Muslims call their Scriptures "the Word of God" is that they believe certain human beings were inspired to utter in human words what God's powerful presence was communicating to them. But as Schneiders points out: "Even to call the Scriptures God's Word (a metaphor) in human words leads very easily to thinking of God's self-gift (revelation) as literal speech. . . .We cannot say that the Bible is purely and simply revelation. It is more correct to say that the Bible is (potentially) revelatory."[13] The reason for her statement is clear: language is a means of communication. For spoken words to be revelatory, they demand listeners: people who are open to the text's transformative power, people who are drawn into the reality of the self-communicating God that the words symbolize. The Bible becomes the actual locus of divine-human encounter only in the act of interpretation.

Karl Barth also makes this same point when he asserts: "Scripture is holy and the Word of God because by the Holy Spirit it became and will become to the Church a witness to divine revelation." This sentence is packed with theological meaning, for it embodies Barth's doctrine of the three-fold Word of God. On its most fundamental level, it refers to God's revelation or personal self-disclosure, which for the Christian has become incarnate in the person of Jesus Christ. In its second form, the Word of God refers to the Spirit-inspired witness of the apostles to the good news of Jesus Christ ("the Gospel") as written down in Holy Scripture. In its third form, it refers to God's Word as proclaimed within the Church. These levels cannot be understood in isolation. As Barth explains, the first, God's self-communication, "is the form that underlies the other two. But it is the very one that never meets us in abstract form. We know it only indirectly, from Scripture and proclamation."[14] Barth's argument here immediately calls to mind two passages from the Johannine writings:

> In the beginning was the Word, and the Word was with God
> . . . .All things came into being through him . . . and the Word
> became flesh and lived among us. . . .No one has ever seen God.
> It is the only Son, God, who is close to the Father's heart, who
> has made him known (John 1: 1-3, 14, 18).

> We declare to you what was from the beginning, what we have
> heard, what we have seen with our eyes, what we have looked
> at and touched with our hands, concerning the word of life—
> this life was revealed, and we have seen it and testify to it, and
> proclaim to you the eternal life that was with the Father and
> revealed to us (1 John 1: 1-2).

What has existed from the beginning is God's plan for creation: that all things might come to have life to the full with God. This plan has been definitively revealed in the person of Jesus Christ, who becomes present in the lives of believers through the testimony of Jesus' disciples. Since we can no longer actually hear those disciples, their witness has been preserved in writings, which in turn become actively present in the proclamation of the faith community. God's Word flows from Christ to the apostles (as written down in Scripture) to the present-day Church—but the order of knowing is reversed: God is revealed in Christ, but Christ is known only through Scripture, and Scripture comes to life only in the present proclamation of the faith community.

This doctrine of the three-fold Word of God has an important implication: namely, that the biblical text does not enjoy an independent status. It does not have an "objective" meaning, divorced from the dynamic of the mediation of God's Word in Christ to the believing community. To say that Scripture *is* the Word of God always refers to an act, an event—it *becomes* God's Word in the assembly of believers who are led to encounter God through its proclamation.[15]

This insight is behind a small but significant liturgical change that occurred only several years ago: namely, that the lector no longer proclaims: "This is the Word of the Lord," often lifting up the lectionary at the same time. Now he or she says: "The Word of the Lord." This change was intended to emphasize that God's Word is not simply *this* text, much less *this* book that contains it, but the proclamation of that Word in this present assembly, a proclamation that demands our response in faith.[16] Revelation is not something that resides in the biblical text itself. Rather, through the work of the Holy Spirit in the Church, an event occurs by which the veil is lifted from the text, by which it comes to witness to

God's self-revelation to us here and now.[17] So it was that Francis believed that preachers "minister to us spirit and life" when they break open "the most holy divine words."[18]

Let us return to Barth's initial questions to those who would approach Scripture: who are you? what are you looking for? For Christians, especially for Franciscans, the answer to the first is: "A person (or community) in search of a deeper life"; to the second, "Christ"—the enlightening and liberating word of God.

This dynamic is illustrated in the stories told about how God "revealed" to Francis that he should "live according to the pattern of the Holy Gospel." Let us look again at the source that contains probably the more accurate scenario of this event. It comes from the *Anonymous of Perugia* (dated to about 1240), and it recounts what happened after two men from Assisi came to Francis, asking if they might join him:

> They told Francis simply: "We wish to live with you from now on and do what you are doing. Tell us therefore what we should do with our possessions." Overjoyed at their coming and their resolve, he answered them kindly, "Let us go and seek counsel from the Lord."
>
> So they went to one of the city's churches. Upon entering it they fell on their knees and humbly prayed: "Lord God, Father of glory, we beg you in your mercy, show us what we are to do." After finishing their prayer, they asked the priest of the church, "Sir, would you show us the Gospel of our Lord Jesus Christ? . . ."
>
> When the priest opened the book, they immediately found the passage, "If you wish to be perfect, go sell everything you possess, and give the money to the poor . . . [then come, follow me]" (Mk 17: 21).
>
> Opening up the book a second time, they discovered, "Whoever wishes to come after me, [must renounce their very self, take up their cross and follow me]" (Mt 16: 24).
>
> When they opened up the book the third time, they came upon: "Take nothing for the journey, [no staff, nor bag . . . nor money]" (Lk 9:3).
>
> When they heard this, they were filled with great joy and exclaimed, "This is what we want. This is what we were seeking." And blessed Francis said, "This will be our Rule."[19]

There are several points in this story that illustrate what I have been saying. First of all, these men believed fervently that they would find

Christ himself in the Scripture. As Francis said, "Let us seek counsel *from the Lord.*" He was convinced that the Gospel text would mediate *Christ's* word to them at this moment. They thus approached the text humbly and in prayer.

But they also brought something to the text: their yearning for a deeper life. As Francis exclaimed: "This is *what we were seeking.*" The passages they encountered that morning did not set them on a new direction, but confirmed how God was already at work in their lives. They were bringing something to their reading of the text, namely the way their lives were being transformed by God's inspiration. Francis had already abandoned all his possessions. His new companions no doubt sensed that they would be called to do the same if they were to "live with Francis and do what he was doing."

Let us also look at Francis's conclusion: "This will be our Rule." What in these texts actually became a Rule? Certainly Francis felt called to enact these passages in a radical way, but contrary to what many in the past have thought, he did not feel impelled to follow the Gospel "literally." Rather, listening to the stories of Jesus' radical obedience to the Father gave him and his companions "signals" for the path they should take in their own lives.[20] It did not mean they felt necessarily called to re-enact all the details in those stories.

Theophile Desbonnets has convincingly demonstrated that even in these famous episodes when Francis discovered a "life according to the Gospels" he did not literally follow everything he heard or read in those accounts.[21] Rather, certain words struck him, spoke to him in a deep way. As he read the Gospel story, he seized on certain words or details in a kind of intuitive grasp of where the Spirit was leading him. In other words, Francis *chose* certain texts as central for him and his brothers. Under the Spirit's inspiration, Francis creatively re-appropriated the Gospel, focusing on certain points as speaking directly to his situation—to himself personally and to his world. Indeed, one can appreciate the truly free and creative nature of Francis and Clare's understanding of the evangelical life when one compares it with many of the other apostolic movements of the time that attempted to copy meticulously biblical norms.

For Francis the Gospel spoke with immediacy and directness. One need only look at the standard medieval exegesis of a Gospel passage central to Francis's vision of a "life according to the Gospel"—the account of Jesus sending his disciples out on mission (Mt. 10:5-23). Here Jesus tells them not to weigh themselves down with a lot of baggage—

but rather to trust in God's providential care. Over the centuries, Christians had allegorized many of the details of this story. By Francis's time, the standard academic biblical commentary, the *Ordinary Gloss*, told readers that gold represents "earthly wisdom which is actually animal and diabolical." Copper coins stand for "evil that has the appearance of good." The money-bag signifies "ill-gotten gains"; two tunics, "duplicity"; the staff, "excessive appetite for power."[22] The text had been reduced to a "spiritual message" that could be applied to any typical congregation. In contrast, on the morning Francis heard that same passage, the words of the Gospel "seemed strangely virginal and new . . . literally unheard of before. That day those words had a meaning."[23]

For Francis, those words spoke directly and deeply. His was not so much a literal reading as a profound reading. These radical Gospel texts forced him to go back to re-evaluate his life and re-orient himself at the root of his being. Francis did not so much follow these Gospel passages "to the letter." Rather he saw *beyond* the letter, that is, according to the Spirit, intuiting something new—"a life according to the Gospel"—from these texts.[24] He and his companions did not interpret the Gospel in a legalistic way, "but with a spiritual dynamism that encourages life and imagination and in a freedom in which new horizons are continually opening out."[25]

Indeed, in what we might call Francis's hermeneutical treatise, his seventh *Admonition*, we can see clearly his emphasis on the spiritual reading of Scripture:

> The apostle says, "The letter kills, but the spirit gives life." Those people are put to death by the letter who only wish to know the words alone, that they might be esteemed wiser than others and be able to acquire great riches. . . .And those religious are put to death by the letter who are not willing to follow the spirit of the divine letter but, instead, wish only to know the words and to interpret them for others. . . .[26]

One cannot remain with a sterile understanding of a word once spoken in the past, but must discover in the letter a fresh message for the present.

Francis's creative reinterpretation of the Gospel in the thirteenth century was actually similar to the approach of contemporary "postmodern" literary scholars who have tried to undermine the idea of a text as an independent meaning-filled entity that presents itself to us simply as an object to be examined—an idea based on the presupposition that the original meaning of the text is the only valid meaning.

Rather, they emphasize that once words are written down as a text, they can generate new meanings. A text has a "surplus" of meaning that can speak in a new way to a reader in a new situation.

H.-G. Gadamer employs the helpful distinction between an art object (the physical entity, such as a painting, a sculpture, or a musical score) and a work of art (that same entity when it is being contemplated or heard). Whereas the art object has continuous existence as a physical identity, the work of art has an intermittent mode of being, actualized when it is being contemplated or heard, a mode of being that can speak to people in many different ways, each of them valid.[27] As Gadamer maintains: "What is fixed in writing has detached itself from the contingency of its origin and made itself free for new relationships. . . .Not occasionally only, but always, the meaning of a text goes beyond its author."[28] A great artist, the poet T. S. Eliot, commented on this phenomenon years ago:

> When a poem has been made, something new has happened, something that cannot be explained by anything that went before. . . .[There is the danger] of assuming that there must be just one interpretation of the poem as a whole that must be "right". . . .But the meaning of the poem as a whole is not exhausted by any explanation, for the meaning is what the poem means to different sensitive readers.[29]

Thus, Eliot explains, we cannot assume that "the interpretation of a poem, if valid, is necessarily an account of what the author consciously or unconsciously was trying to do." Rather, a poem is always a new creation.

> If the word "inspiration" is to have any meaning, it must mean just this, that the speaker or writer is uttering something which he does not wholly understand. . . .A poet may believe that he is expressing only his private experience, . . . yet for his readers what he has written may come to be the expression of their own secret feelings.[30]

The Scriptures as inspired by God's Spirit, then, transcend the conscious intention of the original human author. As read within a community of faith, they have the ability to speak to changed times and changed circumstances, and therefore have a voice that escapes the limitations of the particular circumstances to which they were originally addressed. As Sandra Schneiders puts it, the writings that emerged in the apostolic period and that were incorporated into the biblical canon always remain normative for Christian faith, even though the Church may move "beyond the letter" to new, creative understandings of those texts. Indeed, the understanding of the individuals who originally committed those texts to writing is not necessarily the fullest or the best.

This is the point made in the *Constitution on Divine Revelation* from the Second Vatican Council:

> The tradition that comes from the apostles makes progress in the Church, with the help of the Holy Spirit. There is a growth in insight into the realities and words that are being passed on. This comes about through the contemplation and study of believers who ponder these things in their heart. . . .Thus as the centuries go by, the Church is always advancing toward the plenitude of divine truth until the words of God are fulfilled in her. . . .By means [of this process], the Holy Scriptures are more thoroughly understood and constantly made effective in the Church. Thus God, who spoke in the past, continues to converse with the Spouse of his beloved Son.[31]

Sandra Schneiders presents a helpful analogy to this process. The signers of the Declaration of Independence asserted that "all men are created equal," a phrase that still anchors American democracy. But if we examine the "original intent" of those who composed that phrase, we see that in practice they understood those words to mean free, property-holding white males. It was only through the passage of years, and as a result of bitter struggles, that the full implications of that text were realized with the gradual extension of equal rights to other segments of American society.[32]

The early Franciscan Movement also discovered as yet unexpressed facets of the Gospel message. The brothers and sisters brought something new into the world as they heard old biblical passages in a fresh way. For Francis, the whole biblical message could be condensed into the person of Jesus Christ: "I decided to offer you . . . the words of our Lord Jesus Christ, Who is the Word of the Father, and the words of the Holy Spirit, which are spirit and life."[33]

For Francis, Christ is *the* Word of the Father, and that Word embodied the very nature of God: the Holy One who reaches out in humility toward humanity:

The most high Father made known from heaven through His holy angel Gabriel this Word of the Father—so worthy, so holy and glorious—in the womb of the holy and glorious Virgin Mary, from whose womb he received the flesh of our humanity and frailty. Though He was rich, He wished, together with the most Blessed Virgin, His mother, to choose poverty in the world beyond all else.

And as His passion was near, He celebrated the Passover with His disciples and, taking bread, gave thanks, blessed and broke it, saying: *Take and eat: This is My Body.* And taking the cup He said: *This is My Blood of the New Covenant which will be poured out for you.* . . .He placed His will in the will of His Father, saying: *Father, let Your will be done* . . . His Father's will was such that His blessed and glorious Son, Whom He gave to us and Who was born for us, should offer Himself through His blood as a sacrifice and oblation on the cross . . . for our sins, leaving us an example that we might follow His footprints.[34]

Francis has heard the Scriptures in such a way that their many words have been condensed into the person of Christ, and not all the many possible interpretations of the person of Jesus, but into two episodes—his humble birth and painful death. These captured most vividly for him *the* Word of a humble, self-emptying God.[35] He believed that this was the heart of the Gospel message and it dictated how he was called "to follow his footprints." The three Gospel texts that Francis and his first followers encountered in that church in Assisi all spoke of a radical "denial of self." Like Jesus, his followers had to embody the message of a poor, self-emptying God in this world by a change in their very social condition:

Let all the brothers strive to follow the humility and poverty of our Lord Jesus Christ and let them remember that we should have nothing else in the whole world except, as the Apostle says, having food and clothing, we are content with these. They must rejoice when they live among people considered of little value and looked down upon, among the poor and powerless, the sick and the lepers, and the beggars by the wayside.[36]

Again, near the end of his life, when Francis was in great pain, someone suggested that he might take comfort from hearing passages from the prophets. Francis replied: "It is good to read the testimonies of Scripture, and it is good to see the Lord our God in them. But I have already taken in so much of Scripture that I have more than enough for meditating and reflecting. I do not need more, son; I know Christ—poor and crucified."[37]

These examples illustrate that Francis was not "literally" following Scripture. He had made his choice—to focus his gaze on the poor crucified Christ. Many Christians could, and did, read those same Biblical texts without focusing so intently on the mysteries of the Incarnation and the Passion of Christ. And others, who may have intuited the centrality of those mysteries, did not draw from them a way of following Christ that demanded they actually abandon everything to "live among people considered of little value and looked down upon." The early Franciscan movement read the Gospel in its own, creative way.

Perhaps the most dramatically personal way in which Francis appropriated the Scriptures personally was his reading of the Psalms, which formed the meat of his own personal prayers. We tend sometimes to forget how fundamental the Psalms were for Francis's spirituality. As was customary in his time, it was primarily by means of the Psalter that he would have learned to read, and for years his daily prayer revolved around the Liturgy of the Hours, which he had more or less committed to memory.

In his *Testament*, the terminally ill Francis states: "And although I may be simple and infirm, I nevertheless want to have a cleric always with me who will celebrate the Office for me as it is prescribed in the Rule."[38] His devotion to the Psalms is perhaps best illustrated by an incident later in his life. He was returning to Assisi from Rome, traveling on horseback because of his illness, when it began to rain heavily. Still, when it was time to say his Hours, Francis dismounted and stood along the side of the road in the drenching rain to pray. He said: "If the body wants to eat its food in peace and quiet, and both it and the body eventually will become food for worms, in what peace and quiet should the soul receive its food, which is God Himself!"[39] Francis truly found spirit and life in these ancient prayers.

How did Francis approach these texts? Although he certainly did not study theology in a formal way, his understanding of the Psalms was strikingly similar to that of Augustine. In a truly moving article, Archbishop Rowan Williams shows that, for Augustine, "to read the Psalms is to make our own voice the voice of the Body of Christ."[40] Praying the Psalms is not simply to read the sentiments uttered by some long-ago Hebrew poet: rather, it "unseals deep places" within the believer, "emotions otherwise buried," enabling us to voice our own pain, doubts and fears. The key to Augustine's interpretation of the Psalms was to realize that Christ has identified himself with the struggling members of his Body, the Christian community. And so "Jesus speaks again in the voice of the suffering Christian."[41]

Although we may be tempted to think that God is absent from our lives, yet when we hear Christ utter our words of anguish, we know that God has emptied himself to enter our suffering. "Christ himself is only encountered when we come down to the level at which he has chosen to live, the level of ruined and scarred humanity." The risen Christ not only intercedes for us, but somehow still prays *in* us. In his self-emptying even unto death, "Christ has not only shown the way, but *is* the way."[42]

How integral the Psalms were for Francis is best illustrated by his *Office of the Passion*, a highly original literary composition, that he prayed seven times daily for much of his life.[43] This office is not an arrangement of private devotional prayers but his own creative and entirely personal appropriation of the Psalms and other biblical texts. Each hour of this *Office* begins with a set of praises, drawn from various passages from the Book of Revelation, focusing on the victorious Lamb of God, the risen Christ who has conquered the powers of sin and death.[44] Then each hour contains a psalm, each a pastiche of phrases from various biblical psalms with some additions by Francis. Some psalms voice the supplication of Christ at various stages of his passion; others echo the praises of redeemed humanity to the God who chose to save the world by emptying himself to become human, loving us even unto death on a cross.

> For the Most Holy Father of heaven,
> our King before all ages.
> sent His beloved Son from on high,
> and has brought salvation in the midst of the earth.
>
> Take up your bodies and carry His holy cross
> And follow His most holy commands even to the end.
>
> Let the whole earth tremble before His face
> Tell among the nations
> that the Lord has ruled from a tree.[45]

It was the custom of early monks to have a moment of silence after a psalm and then utter a prayer that summarized its content from the perspective of Christian faith; Francis has creatively drawn on the reso-nances of the Psalms themselves in his memory to accomplish the same thing, but in a more personal and creative manner. What the *Office of the Passion* clearly illustrates is how deeply Scripture was internalized by Francis: its phrases have come to shape his own consciousness, but in a way that the "letter" has truly become alive in his spirit. Francis has become a living word from God.

This article has taken one Franciscan—although a paradigmatic one!—to illustrate how Scripture can make a difference in our lives. With regard to using the Bible in prayer, I have suggested that the great enemy of our spiritual life, when it comes to the Bible, is "the letter"— the idea that these inspired words mean one and only one thing. Both the fundamentalist and the person who relies solely on the historical-critical method to establish one "original" and only valid meaning of a text fall into the same trap. If these sacred texts are not to remain "dead letters" but the living Word of God, we must allow the Spirit room to breathe. Thank God, there are many groups and individuals in the church today who are doing just that—from *comunidades de base* in Latin America, to those who are resurrecting the ancient prayer method of *lectio divina*. The first questions we must ask are not of the text, but of ourselves: who are we? what are we seeking?

Such questions are very much in our Franciscan tradition. In an outstanding work on Francis's reading of Scripture, Walter Egger sum-marized the Franciscan hermeneutic as follows: "Outward respect of God's word; being prepared for conversion; inward poverty in the sight of God." These characteristics define *who* a Franciscan must be when he or she listens to God's Word—a poor, hungry person waiting to be fed. "Putting God's word into effect, the meaning of the text is to be found in action."[46] These qualities illustrate *what* we should be looking for—a message that will change our lives. If these provide the optic in which we hear God's word mediated in the Holy Scriptures, I guarantee you— they will make a difference in our lives and in the world.

Endnotes

[1]"Letter in Response to an Unknown Master," 10, *Works of St. Bonaventure*, Vol. 5: *Writings Concerning the Franciscan Order*, with introduction and translation by Dominic Monti (St. Bonaventure: The Franciscan Institute, 1994), 51.

[2]*The Rule and the General Constitutions of the Order of Friars Minor* (Rome: General Curia, O.F.M., 2004), art. 22, p. 83.

[3]*Dei Verbum*, 25, citing St. Jerome, *Vatican Council II: Constitutions, Decrees, Declara-tions*, ed. Austin Flannery (Northport, NY: Costello Publishing Co., 1996), 114.

[4]I am indebted here to an insightful article by Scott C. Saye, "The Wild and Crooked Tree: Barth, Fish, and Interpretive Communities," *Modern Theology* 12.4 (October, 1996): 435-59.

[5]Karl Barth, *The Word of God and the Word of Man*, trans. Douglas Horton (New York: Harper and Brothers, 1957), 32, as cited in Saye, 436.

[6]*Dei Verbum*, 25, citing St. Ambrose. (Flannery, 114.)

[7]Norbert Nguyen-Van-Khanh, *The Teacher of His Heart: Jesus Christ in the Thought and Writings of St. Francis*, trans. Ed Hagman (St. Bonaventure, NY: The Franciscan Institute, 1994), 189-91.

[8]Nguyen-Van-Khanh, 192.

[9]*Exhortation to the Clergy*, Earlier Edition, 2-3, in *Francis of Assisi: Early Documents*, vol. I, ed. Regis J. Armstrong, J. A. Hellmann and William Short (New York: New City Press, 1999), 52. (Hereafter FAED with corresponding volume number and page.)

[10]*Testament*, 10-13 (FAED I, 125).

[11]Sandra M. Schneiders, *The Revelatory Text: Interpreting the New Testament as Sacred Scripture* (San Francisco: HarperCollins, 1991): 34-35.

[12]Schneiders, 35.

[13]Schneiders, 39.

[14]Karl Barth, *Church Dogmatics*, 4 vols. (Edinburgh: T. and T. Clark, 1956-1975), I/1, 121, as cited in Saye, 443.

[15]Saye, 444.

[16]This proclamation thus parallels the administration of the Eucharist, when the minister proclaims "the Body of Christ." The emphasis is not so much that Christ is present in *this* host, but that the communicant is called to receive the Body of Christ into his or herself and assent to that reality.

[17]Saye, 445.

[18]*Testament*, 13 (FAED I, 125).

[19]*Anonymous of Perugia*, 10 (FAED II, 38).

[20]I owe this image to Patricia Hampl, *Virgin Time: In Search of the Contemplative Life* (New York: Farrar, Straus, Giroux, 1992), 120. Hampl's reference was to later Franciscans' reading of Francis and Clare, but the image also applies to Francis's reading of the Scriptures.

[21]Theophile Desbonnets, "The Franciscan Reading of the Scriptures," in *Francis of Assisi Today*, *Concilium*, vol. 149, ed. Christian Duquoc and Casiano Floristan (New York: The Seabury Press, 1981), 37-45. See also Anton Rotzetter, "Mysticism and Literal Observance of the Gospel in Francis of Assisi," in the same volume, 56-64.

[22]As cited in Desbonnets, 42.

[23]Deteil, cited by Desbonnets, 42.

[24]Deteil, cited by Desbonnets, 43.

[25]Rotzetter, 59.

[26]*Admonition 7*, 1-3 (FAED I, 132).

[27]H.-G. Gadamer, *Truth and Method*, 94-169, as cited in Schneiders, 42.

[28]*Truth and Method*, 357, as cited in Andrew Louth, *Discerning the Mystery: An Essay on the Nature of Theology* (Oxford: The Clarendon Press, 1983), 102-103.

[29]T.S. Eliot, *On Poetry and Poets* (London, New York: Farrar, Straus and Cudahy, 1957), 112, as cited in Louth.

[30]Eliot, 122-123, as cited in Louth, 104-105.

[31]*Dei Verbum*, 8. (Flannery, 102).

[32]Schneiders, 78, 175-76.

[33]*Later Admonition and Exhortation to the Brothers and Sisters of Penance*, 3 (FAED I, 45).

[34]*Later Admonition*, 4-7, 10-13 (FAED I, 46).

[35]In the words of his first biographer, Thomas of Celano, "so thoroughly did the humility of the Incarnation and the charity of the Passion occupy his memory that he scarcely wanted to think of anything else." See *The Life of Saint Francis*, 84 (FAED I, 254).

[36]*Earlier Rule*, 9:1-2 (FAED I, 70).

[37]Thomas of Celano, *The Remembrance of the Desire of a Soul*, 105 (FAED II, 316).

[38]*Testament*, 29 (FAED I, 126).

[39]*Assisi Compilation*, 120 (FAED II, 229).

[40]Rowan Williams, "Augustine and the Psalms," *Interpretation* 58 (2004): 17-27. This quotation is on p. 17.

[41]Williams, 18-19. For Augustine, "two texts are fundamental for all Christian herme-neutics—Jesus' question to Paul on the Damascus Road ('Why are you persecuting me?' Acts 26:15) and the parable of the last judgment, where Jesus identifies himself with 'the least of the brethren' (Matt 25:40)." See Williams, 18.

[42]Williams, 21.

[43]See Dominique Gagnon, "*The Office of the Passion:* The Daily Prayer of Francis of Assisi," in *Greyfriars Review* 7, Supplement (1993): 1-89

[44]Interestingly enough, the reform of the Liturgy of the Hours since Vatican II has followed Francis's intuition by incorporating these canticles from Revelation into Evening Prayer.

[45]*Office of the Passion,* Psalm 7 (FAED I, 147).

[46]W. Egger, *Nachfolge als Weg zum Leben* (Klosterneuberg: n.p., 1979), as cited in Rotzetter, 57.

CHAPTER TWO

A LOVE SUPREME:
THE WRITINGS OF FRANCIS OF ASSISI
AND THE GOSPEL OF JOHN

James P. Scullion, O.F.M.

Introduction

Preconceptions and even prejudices often dictate how we see or hear. The phrase "A Love Supreme" in the title of this article comes neither from a writing of St. Francis of Assisi nor from the Gospel of John, although preconceptions about these writings might impel us to search these works for this phrase. It is, rather, the musical composition of the great jazz saxophonist John Coltrane. Although critics have hailed "A Love Supreme" as a jazz masterpiece, the first-time listener, guided by preconceptions of harmony and rhythm, often hears not an eloquent and sublime piece of music but a strange cacophony of sounds. The discordant or rootless piano chords of McCoy Tyner stretch the hearer's notion of harmony while the pounding and polyrhythmic drumming of Elvin Jones seem to destroy any notion of beat or rhythm. The bleating sound of both John Coltrane's saxophone and his chanting of the refrain "a love supreme" seem less than musical. Such was my experience the first time I listened to this jazz classic as it seemed to stretch the notion of music to the breaking point. Yet like many a classic which is rich and complex, repeated almost obsessive listening and study revealed the depths and beauty of this work. The composition is tightly structured around four movements which Coltrane entitles Acknowledgement, Resolution, Pursuance and Psalm. As these titles indicate, it is a religious work that begins and ends in the praise of God.

A first encounter with Francis's use of the Gospel of John in his writings seems also to reveal a strange cacophony of texts pasted together willy-nilly without any rhyme or reason. Yet like Coltrane's classic, repeated reading and study of the writings of Francis reveal his eloquence, simplicity and inspiration. He does not quote the Gospel in a haphazard fashion but has made the Gospel of John an important source for reflection and prayer.

Let me suggest two further connections between Coltrane's composition "A Love Supreme" and Francis's reading of the Gospel of John.
The first and simplest connection is signaled by Coltrane's title for his
composition, "A Love Supreme," which could well be the title for the
Gospel of John with its emphasis on God's love: "For God so loved the
world that he gave his only Son, so that everyone who believes in him
may not perish but may have eternal life" (John 3:16). The second connection is in the character of the two poets or musicians: both these
figures have been described as mystical and unconventional. Francis of
Assisi was the charismatic and itinerant preacher whose rule and life
was simply the Gospel. John Coltrane was the precursor of "free jazz,"
a jazz that tried to simplify and free itself of the constraints of chord
progressions and fixed rhythms. So both figures were driven to simplify in order to get to the marrow of the music or the Gospel.

A few insights from Coltrane's biography may provide a fresh perspective on Francis, his biography and his writings. First of all, Ashley
Kahn notes in his biography that John Coltrane was a traditionalist. For
a jazz musician, that tradition was the book of standard tunes. There
did not seem to be a song or tune that Coltrane did not know.[1] Although
"A Love Supreme" seems on first hearing to be a cacophony of sounds,
it is, in fact, tunes and modes transformed and transposed. I would
suggest that, in a similar way, Francis was a traditionalist. For Francis
that tradition was the Sacred Scripture, and in his writings those texts
of Sacred Scripture are transformed and transposed into living words.

Coltrane's biography provides a second insight into the musician—
he played and practiced constantly.[2] He learned and composed by doing. So also Francis learned and interpreted the Scripture by doing or,
as Dino Dozzi expresses it, Francis and his first companions read the
gospel by living it ("*leggevano il vangelo per viverlo*").[3]

If you walk around the Upper Church of the Basilica of St. Francis
in Assisi, you see a series of frescos that depict various episodes from
the life of St. Francis. Above these scenes are other frescos depicting
stories from the Old and New Testaments. As you stand there looking
at these frescos, you are seeing and reading the life of St. Francis as he is
reading or incarnating a story from the Sacred Scripture. In a like manner, in this article we want to see and hear Francis as he reads and incar-
nates the Gospel of John. Before we can read and appreciate Francis's
reading of this Gospel, however, we need to be aware of the preconceptions that we bring to our own reading of the Gospel of John since we,
like Francis, always read from a particular context or tradition. These

preconceptions influence how we read and understand John's Gospel. So, before we can look at Francis's medieval reading of the Gospel, we need to reflect on our own modern and postmodern readings of this Gospel of God's love supreme.

Modern Reading of the Gospel of John

The modern reading of the Gospel of John has developed from the application of the historical-critical approach to the study of the Sacred Scripture. Like the modern study of the writings of Francis, this approach sees the text as a window to look through in order to see the sources behind the text, the forms of these sources and the redaction and editing of these sources. Application of this historical-critical approach both to the Scripture and to the writings of Francis also asks about the historical and social context of these texts and their sources.

Many historical critics have discerned a "sign source" behind the Gospel of John. The Evangelist used this sign source as well as other sources to call to faith or to strengthen the faith of the believers: "But these [signs] are written that you may (come to) believe that Jesus is the Messiah, the Son of God, and that through this belief you may have life in his name" (20:31 NAB).[4] Johannine scholars such as Raymond E. Brown suggest that the sources behind the Gospel ultimately go back to the preaching of the Beloved Disciple. The modern consensus is that this disciple was not the apostle John, the son of Zebedee. A figure Brown calls the Evangelist brought together these various sources and the preaching of the Beloved Disciple to form the first edition of the Gospel. The Gospel was "completed" by a redactor who expanded the work of the Evangelist with additions to the Last Supper discourse (chaps. 15-17) as well as adding a second ending (chap. 21).[5]

Both Raymond E. Brown and J. Louis Martyn have studied the historical and social context of the Fourth Gospel. They argue that the Gospel must be read on two levels: (1) as the story of Jesus and (2) as the story of the Johannine community.[6] Martyn provides a detailed analysis of the expansive story of the man born blind in John 9. On one level this chapter reflects the healing ministry of the historical Jesus (9:1-8) but the expansion of this miracle story brings in the story of the Johannine community and its growing conflict with Judaism (9:8-41).[7] This growing tension with Judaism is reflected in the Evangelist's comment that the ". . . Jews had already agreed that anyone who confessed Jesus to be the Messiah would be put out of the synagogue" (9:22, 34). The "parting of the ways" or separation from the synagogue reflects the situation not of the historical Jesus in the 30s but of the Johannine community in the mid 80s.

The modern study of the Gospel of John strives to interpret the Gospel within its proper historical context. It should be noted, however, that the first interpretive move of placing the text into its proper historical context also distances the text from the modern interpreter. This may seem to make it irrelevant since it no longer addresses the situation of the modern community but rather the situation of the Johannine community of the first century.

Postmodern Reading of the Gospel of John

If the modern interpreter of the Gospel of John wishes to see through the Gospel to the situation of the Johannine community, a postmodern approach wishes to enter into dialogue with the text itself. Methods such as narrative criticism and reader-response criticism can be loosely categorized as postmodern readings of John.[8] Narrative criticism focuses not on the sources or history behind the text but on the text itself and employs a close and detailed analysis of the text, its plot, characters and conflicts. Reader-response criticism sees the reader or hearer as a co-creator of the text. The text is a musical score to be performed and each performance will be different. Thus, in true postmodern fashion, these approaches emphasize dialogue or interaction with the text and stress polyvalency or multiple readings of the same text.

A narrative approach to John would focus on the story itself and the parallels or contrasts between the characters within the narrative. So, for example, both Nicodemus (2:23-3:21) and the Samaritan woman (4:1-42) have an initial encounter with Jesus that begins with misunderstanding but ends differently. Nicodemus comes to Jesus at night but, since he cannot even understand "earthly things" (3:12), he never comes into the light. The Samaritan woman begins on an earthly level (4:11-12) but comes to a deeper understanding of Jesus and becomes a missionary who brings many people from her city to faith in Jesus through her testimony (4:39). The passage ends with the Samaritans declaring that Jesus is the Savior of the world (4:42).

In a similar way, a narrative approach would contrast the character of the paralytic who is healed in chapter 5 with the man born blind who is healed in chapter 9. Both are healed on the Sabbath (5:9; 9:14) and both are questioned by the Jewish authorities (5:12; 9:15, 21). The paralytic reports Jesus to the Jewish authorities, whereas the man born blind proclaims his faith in Jesus as Lord and worships him (5:15; 9:38).

The interpretive moves of narrative and reader-response criticism tend to make the text more relevant because they involve the reader in the story so that the distance between the text and reader is bridged through this dialogue. These approaches help to avoid what might be termed the etymological fallacy, the mistaken notion that knowing the etymology behind a word necessarily gives us the true meaning of the word. In a similar way, knowing the sources behind a text does not necessarily give us the meaning of the text.

Reader-response criticism is important for both a postmodern as well as a medieval reading of the Gospel of John since it places value on multiple readings of the same text. This approach values the reading not only of a world-renowned Johannine biblical scholar such as Raymond E. Brown, but also the reading of a poor and humble servant of God such as Francis of Assisi.

This review of modern and postmodern reading traditions is important because we are children of our age or ages. Even if we have never taken a course in exegesis or the Gospel of John, we still experience these methods and approaches through the homilies that we hear, the ecclesial or spiritual reading that we do and the Bible study groups in which we participate. They are the preconceptions we bring when we read the Gospel.

As we turn now to place Francis into his interpretive tradition, it is important to keep in mind that he assimilated his interpretive strategy in a similar way. He was not a professional exegete. There is no evidence he studied Scripture or theology in a formal way. His Scriptural knowledge was formed through the sermons that he heard and through his meditation on the reading of the Gospel and the Divine Office.[9]

Medieval Readings of the Gospel of John

Francis, as a child of the Middle Ages, inherited many of its preconceptions about the Gospel of John (such as authorship by the apostle John, the son of Zebedee). Medieval interpretation, although premodern or precritical, still sought a detailed analysis of the text in an attempt to apply it to the contemporary situation. This medieval reading was heir to two different currents or approaches of patristic exegesis—the literal and the allegorical.

A good example of a detailed and literal interpretation of this Gospel is found in John Chrysostom's *Homilies on the Gospel of St. John*. While usually ending these sermons with practical moral advice and exhortations, he did not avoid an exacting examination of the meaning of Greek words, particularly when he was combating Christological errors.[10] The other and more influential patristic interpreter was Augustine. The key exegetical principle for Augustine was love. Love alone enables one to comprehend the spiritual meaning of a text. An interpretation that does not foster the double love of God and neighbor does not understand the text.[11] Augustine's exegetical approach at times made use of elaborate allegories to penetrate the spiritual meaning of the text. In his interpretation of the wedding feast at Cana, for example, he provides an allegorical interpretation for each of the six stone jars (John 2:6)—they "signify the six eras in which prophecy was not lacking."[12]

Most priests and preachers of the Middle Ages would not have read the actual commentaries of the great patristic exegetes. Nevertheless, their influence was still felt through the *Glossa Ordinaria*, a work that provided biblical texts with summaries of patristic commentaries, especially those of Augustine and Jerome.[13] These modes of interpretation would eventually filter down to St. Francis as he learned to read by memorizing the Psalms, as he listened to sermons and as he came into contact with ecclesiastical officials such as Pope Innocent III.

St. Francis's Reading of the Gospel of John

As we survey and study Francis's reading and interpretation of the Gospel of John, we need to remember that he was not an exegete but one who interpreted or incarnated the word by doing. His writings take various forms: admonitions and exhortations, rules, letters and prayers. We do not have a commentary *per se* on the Gospel of John. We know that Francis preached not only by actions but also by words; yet among his writings we do not have a copy of any sermons. Perhaps the closest we come are his *Admonitions,* which can be viewed as "mini-sermons" since they often began by citing a Scripture text and then moved to an exhortation. Yet in spite of this dearth of formal biblical commentaries, his admonitions, letters and rules are replete with quotations and allusions to the Gospel of John as well as to the rest of Scripture.

Besides explicit citations of John's Gospel, the writings of Francis also reveal the importance of Johannine titles and images in the formation of Francis's own image of God, of Jesus and of himself. In John 17 Jesus addresses God as "holy Father." Francis often uses this title for God in his own writings (*pater sancta*, PrsG 1; OfP 1:5, 9; 4:9; 5:9; 6:12; ER 22:45; 23:1; 1LtF 1:14; 2LtF 56). This title captures both God's transcendence and immanence. Since what is holy is that which is separated,

God is wholly other. At the same time, the title Father brings out God's familial closeness.

Many of the titles that Francis uses for Jesus also sound Johannine even if no specific text from the Gospel is cited. Among these titles are Good Shepherd (10:11, 14; 1Frg 19; Adm 6:1; ER 22:32), Beloved Son of the Father, Word of the Father (2LtF 3, 4), Apostle of the Father, Christ, Way, truth, life.[14] Finally Francis's own image of himself as servant seems to be inspired by Jesus' service of washing feet at the Last Supper (13:1-20; cf. ER 6:3; Adm 4:2).[15]

We will examine three writings of Francis in which he cites and interprets the Gospel of John. First we will study *Admonition* 1, which can be viewed as a "mini-homily" on John 14:6-9. Next we will study the *Earlier Rule*, particularly Chapter 22, which contains an extensive quotation from John 17. Finally we will study the *Earlier Exhortation to the Brothers and Sisters of Penance*, which, like the *Earlier Rule,* cites the so-called "high priestly prayer" from John 17.

Admonition 1

The *Admonitions* of St. Francis can be viewed as "mini-homilies" since most of them begin with an explicit citation of Scripture, often introduced with the formula "the Lord said/says" (*dicit Dominus*): 1:1; 3:1; 4:1; 9:1). The text then moves from citation and interpretation to exhortation or admonition.

The topic of *Admonition* 1 is given in the heading: "On the Body of the Lord." It quotes extensively from John (14:6-9; 4:24; 1:18; 6:64, 65; 9:35; 1:18). Norbert Nguyên-Van-Khanh argues that the historical context for this admonition was the Eucharistic crisis in the Middle Ages. Because of moral and religious laxity as well as extreme fear and respect, the faithful were no longer receiving the Eucharist on a regular basis.[16] The *Admonition* ends with the exhortation: ". . . let us, as we see bread and wine with our bodily eyes, see and firmly believe (*videamus et credamus firmiter*) that they are His most holy Body and Blood living and true" (Adm 1:21). This exhortation brings out the close connection between "seeing and believing," a key Johannine theme (John 20: 24-29).

The *Admonition* begins with a full citation from John 14:6-9. This section of John is part of Jesus' Last Supper discourse (John 13-17). At the beginning and end of chapter 14, Jesus tells his disciples: "Do not let your hearts be troubled" (vv. 1, 27). Between these comforting words,

Jesus and his disciples engage in a series of questions and responses. Jesus tells the disciples that he is going away but that they know the "way to the place where I am going" (v. 4). Francis begins his citation where Jesus answers Thomas's question: "Lord, we do not know where you are going. How can we know the way?" The quotation in the *Admonition* begins by changing the addressee of Jesus' response. It is now addressed to the disciples (*dicit Dominus Jesus discipulis suis*) instead of just to Thomas (*dicit ei Iesus*). This interpretive change in the text gives it a wider application.

Jesus tells the disciples that he is the "way, the truth, and the life" (John 14:6; Adm 1:1). This quotation from John 14:6-9 emphasizes knowing and seeing the Father. If one sees Jesus one sees the Father (*qui videt me, videt et Patrem*). Francis then cites two other Johannine texts to show that God is spirit (John 4:24) and that [therefore] no one has ever seen God (John 1:18). The only and true way to see God is in the Spirit. There is a contrast between seeing "spiritually" and seeing "physically" (Adm 1: 6; John 6:63). So too with "seeing" Jesus: true seeing is "spiritual seeing" not according to "humanity" but "according to the Spirit and the Divinity." Those who do not "see and believe" spiritually but only according to the humanity are condemned (Adm 1:8). The point of Francis's citation and interpretation of these Johannine texts is reached in the next line: "Now in the same way, all those who see the sacrament . . . in the form of bread and wine . . . and who do not see and believe according to the Spirit and the Divinity (*non vident et credunt secundum spiritum et divinitatem*) that it is truly the Body and Blood of our Lord Jesus Christ, are condemned" (Adm 1:9).

The first chapter of the *Admonitions* challenges one to see the Son and the Eucharist not only physically but also spiritually. A spirituality that moves from the physical to the spiritual is clearly at the core of a Franciscan spirituality. This text from the *Admonitions* shows how this Franciscan spirituality is rooted in a Johannine spirituality. The miracles in John's Gospel are signs that challenge one to move from the physical to the spiritual level. It is important to note that for the Gospel, as also for Francis, the world and the physical are neither evil nor something that has to be blocked out to reach God. Just the opposite: each is a sacrament, a sign that points to and leads one to the divine.

Earlier Rule: Chapter 22

When we come to study the Rules of St. Francis it is somewhat surprising that the *Later Rule* lacks any explicit citation of the Gospel of John.

In this respect it is not all that different from the Rule of St. Benedict.[17] In contrast, chapter 22 of the *Earlier Rule* contains a number of quotations or allusions (John 14:23; 4:23-24; 15:7; 6:64; 14:6; 12:28) as well as an extensive quotation from John 17 (ER 22:41-55). In addition, there are some ten scattered quotations or allusions to the Gospel of John throughout other parts of the *Earlier Rule*.[18] The importance of chapter 22 and Francis's use of John 17 requires further scrutiny.

Chapter 22, "An Admonition to the Brothers," occurs immediately before a chapter on "Prayer and Thanksgiving" and the concluding chapter. Immediately before chapter 22, Francis calls upon the brothers to "announce this or similar exhortation or praise among all people" (21:1), ending with a blessing on those who do penance and a woe on those who do not do penance (21:7-8).

Chapter 22, therefore, occupies an important position within the *Rule*. Both its placement and content suggest that it provides a synthesis of Francis's understanding of the Gospel.[19] As part of this synthesis Francis cites extensively and in order from John 17, specifically vv. 1, 6, 8-10, 11, 13-15, 17-20, 23, 24, 26. The context for this citation is an exhortation: "Let us, therefore, hold onto the words, the life, the teaching and the Holy Gospel (*verba, vitam et doctrinam et sanctum eius evangelium*, 22:41). As Dino Dozzi suggests, these words form an *inclusio* with the beginning of the *Rule*: "The rule and life of these brothers is this . . . to follow the teaching and footprints of our Lord Jesus Christ" (*Regula et vita istorum fratrum haec est, . . . et Domini nostri Jesu Christi doctrinam et vestigia sequi* 1:1). So the rule and life is the Holy Gospel.[20]

This Holy Gospel is summarized by Jesus' prayer for his disciples (John 17:1-26). Although he omits some verses, Francis provides an extensive quotation from this prayer to conclude this exhortation. This selective citation from John 17 highlights three aspects of the Gospel: the Gospel as revelation, as mission and as promise. It is revelation: Jesus has revealed God's name and word(s) to his disciples (22:42-50; John 17:6, 8-11, 13-15). It is mission: as God has sent Jesus into the world, Jesus now sends his disciples into the world (22:51-54; John 17:17-20). Finally, it is promise: Jesus' prayer and wish is that the disciples may be where Jesus is and see God's glory and kingdom (22:55; John 17:24; Matt. 20:21). Francis makes Jesus' prayer for his disciples his own prayer for his brothers. The Rule and life of the friars is the Gospel: it is a word of revelation, a call to mission and a word of promise.

Earlier Exhortation to the Brothers and Sisters of Penance

The final text we will examine is from the *Earlier Exhortation* or *First Letter to the Faithful*. It is both an exultation over those who do penance (1:1-19) and an exhortation to those who do not do penance (2:1-22). Leonhard Lehmann, in his detailed study of this text, notes its "affinity above all with chapter 21" of the *Earlier Rule*.[21] This affinity also extends to chapter 22, since it too makes explicit and extensive use of Jesus' "high priestly prayer" from the Gospel of John.

In this *Earlier Exhortation*, Francis, like Moses before him (Deut. 11:26-29), sets before the brothers and sisters a blessing and a curse. Francis proclaims (1:5) "happy and blessed" (*O quam beati et benedicti*) those who do penance, that is, those who love the Lord and their neighbors, who hate their vices and sins, who receive the Eucharist and who do fruits of penance (1:1-4). Those who do not do penance are cursed. They are children of the devil, "whose works they do" (2:9, 6; John 8:41, 44).

The first chapter is a prayer that begins with the sign of the cross and ends with Amen (1:19). The prayer blesses those who do penance. They are children (*filii*) of the heavenly Father and spouses (*sponsi*), brothers (*fratres*) and mothers (*matres*) of the Lord Jesus Christ (1:7-10). They are children because they do the works of the Father. They are spouses when they are joined to Christ by the Holy Spirit, brothers when they do the will of the Father and mothers when they carry Christ and give birth to him through holy activity (*per sanctam operationem*).

In the context of the prayer that is this chapter, Francis adopts once again and makes his own Jesus' prayer for his disciples. After another series of exultations over the Father and Lord Jesus (1:11, 12, 13), Francis echoes John 10:15, describing Jesus as the one who laid down His life for his sheep and prayed to his Father (1:13).

Francis cites Jesus' prayer verbatim from John 17 although he leaves out some verses. The citation follows the verse order of the Gospel with the exception that verse 11 is moved up to the beginning of the prayer invoking God as "Holy Father" (*Pater sancta*). As in the *Earlier Rule* 22, Francis cites extensively from Jesus' prayer in John 17. Whereas the *Earlier Rule* cites verses 1, 6, 8-10, 11, 13-15, 17-20, 23-24, 26, the *Earlier Exhortation* cites verses 11, 6, 8, 9, 17, 19, 20, 23-24. Both the *Earlier Rule* and the *Earlier Exhortation* conclude with a conflation of the Gospels of John and Matthew and an Amen: "I wish, Father, that where I am, they also may be with me that they may see my glory (John 17:24) in your kingdom. Amen (1:19; Matt 20:21; cf. ER 22:55).

The Gospel of John is of central importance for the continuity and unity of the *Earlier Exhortation*. More specifically, John 17 forms the "very marrow" of this text.[22] Francis once again appropriates this prayer and makes Jesus' prayer for his disciples his own prayer for the brothers and sisters of penance. When one compares this citation with that in the *Earlier Rule*, one notes that they both speak of the Gospel as revelation and as promise. They differ in that the *Earlier Exhortation* does not include the notion of mission since, unlike the *Earlier Rule*, it omits John 17:18: "As You sent me into the world, so I sent them into the world" (ER 22:51).

Conclusions and Implications

The purpose of this study was to explore how Francis read and prayed the Gospel of John. While Francis cites many sections from this Gospel, the key chapters that he returns to again and again are John 6 (1LtCus 6; Adm 1:6, 11; 1LtF 2:21; 2Ltf 3, 23; 1Frg 25; ER 20:5; 22:39; Test 13), John 14 (Adm 1:1-4; 1LtF 1:6; 2LtF 48; 1Frg 16, 26; ER 22:27, 40) and preeminently John 17. As one observes Francis reading this Gospel, one notices that he makes the prayers of Jesus his own. He does not just read the Gospel but prays the Gospel.

Prayer can be defined in many different ways. If we develop a definition for prayer using the key categories of Old Testament Psalms, praise and lament, we can define prayer as an affirming and challenging encounter with the living God. Scripture not only models for us how to praise God but also how to challenge God: "My God, my God, why have you forsaken me?" (Ps. 22:1). Similarly, praying the Scripture should both affirm and challenge ourselves as individuals and as a community. An examination of Francis at prayer, particularly as he reads and prays the Gospel of John, should likewise affirm and challenge the way we pray and the way we read this Gospel. Francis "models" for us how to make Jesus' prayer our own.

Francis ends his *Earlier Exhortation* with a final plea: "In the love (*in caritate*) which is God we beg all those whom these words reach to receive those fragrant words of our Lord Jesus Christ written above with divine love (*cum divino amore*) and kindness" (1LtF 2:19). In harmony with Augustine's exegetical principle of love, Francis's reading and praying of the Gospel of John begins and ends with the love of God. When we listen to John Coltrane's musical composition, "Love Supreme," our notion of the elements of music, harmony and rhythm is expanded and stretched almost to the breaking point. In a similar way, when we listen to Francis reading and praying the Gospel of John, our image of ourselves and especially of God is stretched so that we can truly encounter the One who is Love Supreme.

Bibliography

Armstrong, Regis J. "'If My Words Remain in You . . .': Foundations of the Evangelical Life." *Francis of Assisi: History, Hagiography and Hermeneutics in the Early Documents.* Hyde Park, NY: New City Press, 2004. 68-69.

Brown, Raymond E. *An Introduction to the Gospel of John.* The Anchor Bible Reference Library. Ed. Francis J. Moloney. New York: Doubleday, 2003.

Culpepper, R. Alan. *Anatomy of the Fourth Gospel: A Study in Literary Design.* Philadelphia: Fortress, 1983.

Dozzi, Dino. *Il Vangelo nella Regola non Bollata di Francesco d'Assisi.* Bibliotheca Seraphico Capuccina 36. Rome: Istituto Storico dei Cappuccino, 1989.

Flood, David and Thaddée Matura. *The Birth of a Movement: A Study of the First Rule of St. Francis.* Chicago: Franciscan Herald Press, 1975.

Fortna, Robert T. *The Gospel of Signs.* Society for New Testament Studies Monograph Series. Vol. 11. Cambridge: Cambridge University, 1970.

Francis of Assisi: Early Documents. Vol. I. *The Saint.* Ed. Regis Armstrong, Wayne Hellmann and William Short. New York: New City Press, 1999.

Kahn, Ashley. *A Love Supreme: The Story of John Coltrane's Signature Album.* New York, Viking Press, 2002.

Kealy, Seán P. *John's Gospel and the History of Biblical Interpretation.* Mellen Biblical Press Series 60a, 60b. Lewiston, NY: Mellen Press, 2002.

Lehmann, Leonhard. "Exultation and Exhortation to Penance: A Study of the Form and Content of the *First Version of the Letter to the Faithful.*" *Greyfriars Review* 4.2 (1990): 1-33.

Martyn, J. Louis. *History and Theology in the Fourth Gospel.* The New Testament Library. 3rd ed. Louisville, KY: Westminster John Knox, 2003.

Nguyên-Van-Khanh, Norbert. *The Teacher of His Heart: Jesus Christ in the Thought and Writings of St. Francis.* St. Bonaventure, NY: The Franciscan Institute, 1994.

Schlauri, Ignace. "Saint François et la Bible: Essai Bibliographique de sa Spiritualité Évangélique." *Collectanea Franciscana* 40 (1970): 365-437.

Smalley, Beryl. *The Study of the Bible in the Middle Ages*. Notre Dame, IN: University of Notre Dame Press, 1978.

Soulen, Richard N. and R. Kendall Soulen. *Handbook of Biblical Criticism*. 3rd ed. Louisville, KY: Westminster John Knox, 2001.

Stibbe, Mark W. G. *John as Storyteller: Narrative Criticism and the Fourth Gospel*. Society for New Testament Studies Monograph Series. Vol. 73. Cambridge: Cambridge University, 1992.

Van Asseldonk, Optato. "San Giovanni Evangelista negli Scritti di S. Francesco." *Laurentianum* 18 (1977): 225-55.

Endnotes

[1] Ashley Kahn, *A Love Supreme: The Story of John Coltrane's Signature Album* (New York, Viking Press, 2002), 72.

[2] Kahn, 8.

[3] Dino Dozzi, *Il Vangelo nella Regola non Bollata di Francesco d'Assisi*, Biblioteca Seraphico Capuccina, 36 (Roma: Istituto Storico dei Cappuccini, 1989), 48.

[4] Unless otherwise indicated as here, Scripture texts will be taken from the NRSV.

[5] Raymond E. Brown, *An Introduction to the Gospel of John*, The Anchor Bible Reference Library, ed. Francis J. Moloney (New York: Doubleday, 2003), 74-85, 189-98.

[6] Brown, 75-77; J. Louis Martyn, *History and Theology in the Fourth Gospel*, 3rd edition, The New Testament Library (Louisville: Westminster John Knox Press, 2003), 30-32.

[7] Martyn, 35-66.

[8] Richard N. Soulen and R. Kendall Soulen, *Handbook of Biblical Criticism*, 3rd edition (Louisville: Westminster John Knox Press, 2001), 140-42.

[9] Dozzi, 51-55.

[10] Seán P. Kealy, *John's Gospel and the History of Biblical Interpretation*, Mellen Biblical Press Series 60a, 60b (Lewiston, NY: Mellen Press, 2002), 71-73.

[11] Kealy, 87.

[12] *Tract. Ev. Jo.* 9.6.3, in *St. Augustine: Tractates on the Gospel of John 1-10*, trans. John W. Rettig, The Fathers of the Church (Washington, DC: Catholic University of America Press, 1988), 54.

[13] Beryl Smalley, *The Study of the Bible in the Middle Ages* (Notre Dame, IN: University of Notre Dame Press, 1978), 46-66; Kealy, 140-42.

[14] Optatus Van Asseldonk, "San Giovanni Evangelista negli Scritti di S. Francesco," *Laurentianum* 18 (1977): 228.

[15] All translations of Francis's writings are taken from *Francis of Assisi: Early Documents*, vol. I, *The Saint*, ed. Regis J. Armstrong, J. A. Wayne Hellmann and William J. Short (New York: New City Press, 1999). Abbreviations of the names of individual writings are also taken from this volume. The Latin text is taken from *Opuscula Sancti Patris Francisci Assisiensis*, ed. Kajetan Esser (Grottaferrata: Collegii S. Bonaventurae ad Claras Aquas, 1976). The Latin text is available online at: http://www.franciscanos.org/esfa/menud1.html.

[16] Norbert Nguyên-Van-Khanh, *The Teacher of His Heart: Jesus Christ in the Thought and Writings of St. Francis* (St. Bonaventure, NY: The Franciscan Institute, 1994), 153-56.

[17] With respect to the Rule of Benedict, Kealy notes that only eight quotations from John's Gospel are found, although a "Johannine atmosphere permeates the whole of the Rule" (Kealy, 110).

[18]In addition to chapter 22, quotations from or allusions to the Gospel of John are found in 6:3 (John 13:14); 8:7 (12:6); 9:4 (11:27); 11:5 (15:12); 16:7 (3:5); 16:13 (15:20); 20:5 (6:55); 21:8 (8:41); 23:1 (17:11); 23:3 (17:26).

[19]Regis J. Armstrong, "'If My Words Remain in You . . .': Foundations of the Evangelical Life," *Francis of Assisi: History, Hagiography and Hermeneutics in the Early Documents* (Hyde Park, NY: New City Press, 2004), 68-69; Dozzi, 270-88;

[20]Dozzi, 271.

[21]Leonhard Lehmann, "Exultation and Exhortation to Penance: A Study of the Form and Content of the *First Version of the Letter to the Faithful,*" *Greyfriars Review* 4.2 (1990): 25. He suggests (p. 5) a threefold structure: Exultation (1:1-19), Exhortation (2:1-18) and Postscript (2:19-22). The postscript states the letter should be read aloud and observed.

[22]Lehmann, 18, 16.

CHAPTER THREE

ST. BONAVENTURE'S CHRISTOLOGY AND TEACHINGS ON THE EVANGELICAL LIFE IN HIS *Commentary on the Gospel of Luke*

Robert J. Karris, O.F.M.

Introduction

My assignment is to explore Bonaventure's Christology and teachings about the evangelical life in his *Commentary on the Gospel of Luke*, which dates to ca. 1265, runs to 600 double-column pages in Latin, and 2,459 pages in English translation.[1] That is, I am not looking at the Christology that Bonaventure propounds in Book III of his *Sentence Commentary*.[2] Nor am I investigating the perspectives he offers on the spiritual life in his *De triplici via*. While my goal is, therefore, precise, it is not easy, for Luke's Gospel itself offers its own Christology and teachings about the spiritual life. In presenting Luke's teachings about the Lord Jesus and about the spiritual life, might Bonaventure be simply repeating Luke and not making his own singular contributions? Again might Bonaventure be introducing non-Lukan teachings into the text? On the other hand, might Bonaventure reveal his interpretive hand by the emphases he places on certain aspects of Luke's Christology and view of the spiritual life? That is, Bonaventure may not be smuggling themes into Luke's Gospel, but underlining some that are there and downplaying others.

I try to get inside these interpretive or hermeneutical issues by first presenting the way in which Bonaventure accentuates Luke's high Christology of Jesus, God and human, Son of God. Then I quickly handle two christological points that Bonaventure makes, based on a reading of the text, but that do not dominate his commentary: Jesus as Center and Jesus as Beginning and Fountain of Wisdom. My major presentation will consist of presenting Bonaventure's emphasis on 2 Corinthians 8:9[3] and contrasting it with that of a contemporary Roman Catholic commentator, Brendan Byrne.[4] While Byrne's approach accentuates the thematic of hospitality in Luke's Gospel, Bonaventure emphasizes poverty and humility. For Byrne Jesus Christ is the hospitality of God. For Bonaventure Jesus Christ is God's poverty and humility.[5] In a second part, I deal with Bonaventure's view of the evangelical life and apologize in advance for any overlap between this section and the previous one. In a third and final part I raise the question of what may have prompted Bonaventure and Byrne to put the emphasis on Luke's Christology and view of evangelical life where they did.

Part I

Bonaventure's Christology

Bonaventure's Emphasis on Jesus as Son of God

Joseph A. Fitzmyer notes the following christological titles in Luke's Gospel: Messiah, Lord, Savior, Son of God, Son of Man, Servant, Prophet, King, Son of David, Leader, Holy One, Righteous One, Judge and Teacher.[6] As far as I can determine, Bonaventure's emphasis falls squarely on Jesus, God incarnate or Son of God, as the primary Lukan christological title. I give two major examples from many. In describing Levi's leaving all to follow Christ, Bonaventure comments, quoting Jerome, with whom he agrees:

> For he had seen Christ's miracles. For this reason Jerome says that "the brightness of the hidden divinity, which shone on the human face of Christ, could draw, immediately and with one look, those who looked upon him. Just as it is said that there is power in a lodestone to draw to itself and join together both rings and straw, so too and with greater power could the Lord of creatures draw to himself those he wanted."[7]

A second example stems from Bonaventure's extensive exposition of Luke 20:44 ("David calls him Lord"):

> And further, since David was a glorious king, it does not seem that he would have some mere human as lord. Wherefore, the resolution is this: since Christ, who had the identical nature as King David, could not be said to be true son and lord at the same time, it is necessary that he himself is God and man at the same time. . . .For in this is the foundation of the Christian reli-

gion, in which everything to be believed is rooted and enclosed, namely, that Christ should be believed to be man and God. For all articles of faith are reduced to either his divinity or his humanity.[8]

Almost as an aside, I note that since Bonaventure accentuates Jesus as God and human or as Son of God, he has great difficulty dealing with the non-belief of the Jews, who should have seen Jesus as divine because of his miracles. In his exegesis of Luke 11:31, Bonaventure contrasts the queen of the South with the Jews:

She, of the weak sex, comes from a remote territory, with difficulty, having left her kingdom, with gifts, to a mere man, known only by reputation, as is expressly garnered from 1 Kings 10:1-10. But for the Jews: men who contemn and despise Christ present, freely revealing himself, unique, beneficent, God and man, proved by miracles.[9]

In commenting on Luke 11:32, Bonaventure contrasts the Ninevites' repentance at Jonah's preaching to the Jews' largely negative response to Christ:

But Christ showed greater things than these to the Jews. Therefore, the text adds: And behold, a greater than Jonah is here. For Christ was not only man, but also and truly God, which he showed by the magnitude of his miracles. He did not preach for a few days, but for three years. Therefore, the hardness of the unbelieving Jews is greatly condemned.[10]

In brief, the miracles of Christ, God and human, should have convinced the Jews.

Bonaventure's View of Christ as Mediator and Center

Those of us who have been nourished by Zachary Hayes's *The Hidden Center*[11] would be surprised if we didn't discover some reference to Christ as Mediator and Center in Bonaventure's voluminous *Commentary on the Gospel of Luke*. Bonaventure does not disappoint us. I give two examples that are somehow based on the Lukan text. In expounding on the meaning of Luke 4:30, "But he, passing through their midst, went his way," Bonaventure states:

Through the middle he goes, because, as "mediator between God and human beings" (1 Timothy 2:5), he always loves the center. Thus John 1:26 has: "Your center has stood, whom you do not know."[12]

As Hayes observes:

The concept of the center (= *medium*) is the basis for the office of the incarnate Word as Mediator. . . .The historical mediatorship of Christ is grounded in the inner-trinitarian reality of the second person. He alone can be a mediator who is a *medium*.[13]

A second example of Christ as Center occurs in Bonaventure's exegesis of Luke 24:36:

Now when they were talking about these things, Jesus stood in the middle of them and said to them: Peace be to you. He stood in the middle of them, for he is the mediator. 1 Timothy 2:5 reads: "The mediator between God and human beings is the human Christ Jesus." And therefore, John 1:26 states: "Your center has stood, whom you do not know. . . ." Now he said: Peace to you, because he himself is the peacemaker.[14]

Jesus as the Beginning and Fountain of all Wisdom

In his exposition of Luke 11:31 Bonaventure states:

Indeed, by saying *a greater than Solomon*, he shows that not only is he to be believed as a wise man, but as the beginning and fountain of all wisdom, according to what John 8:25 has: "I am the beginning, who is speaking to you."[15]

Here Bonaventure employs his unique reading of John 8:25, which normally reads "What I have said to you from the beginning," to make his high christological point that Christ is the beginning.[16] And Bonaventure continues:

For Christ was greater than Solomon by reason of his power, knowledge, and justice. Therefore, what this Psalm says is very fitting for him: "O God, give to the king your judgment" (71:1). The Jews believed this Psalm to have been composed in praise of Solomon, when it was said therein: "He will rule from sea to sea" (verse 8). And again: "His name outlasts the sun, and in him all the tribes of the earth will be blessed" (verse 17). Solomon was a temporal peacemaker, but Christ an eternal. Isaiah 9:7

reads: "His rule will be multiplied." He was wise, but Christ is Wisdom. 1 Corinthians 1:24 has: "Christ, the power and wisdom of God." And Colossians 2:3 says: "In whom are hidden all the treasures of wisdom and knowledge." He effected justice, but he was justice itself. 1 Corinthians 1:30 states: "who has become for us God-given justice," etc.[17]

Bonaventure's Major Image of Christ as One Who Gave Up Riches and Became Poor to Enrich Us (2 Corinthians 8:9)

In the course of publishing my annotated translation of *Bonaventure's Commentary on the Gospel of Luke*, I insisted that each volume have an index and that the final volume have a cumulative index of all three volumes. As a matter of fact, I personally compiled the index for volume one. If you were to check the cumulative indices in volume three, you would eventually discover that 2 Corinthians 8:9 is one of Bonaventure's most frequently cited passages and is quoted ten times.[18] To highlight Bonaventure's interpretation and use of 2 Corinthians 8:9, I contrast his exposition with that of Brendan Byrne.

Luke 2:1-7: The Birth of Jesus

Bonaventure's postill on the birth of Jesus is so rich that I can only quote a few snippets from it. I invite my readers to see how Bonaventure builds upon elements in the Lukan text. Relative to Jesus' mother, Mary, Bonaventure comments:

> . . . the text points to the poverty of the one giving birth, because she lacks clothing, a bed, and hospitality. With regard to the paucity of clothing it says: *And she wrapped him in swaddling clothes*, that is, not in one single garment, but in many, so that he could be called a pauper in tatters and would clearly exemplify what the Apostle says in 1 Timothy 6:8: "Having some food and something in which we are clothed, let us be content with these."[19]

With regard to the manger Bonaventure observes:

> And because of the lack of a bed the text continues: *She laid him in a manger*, not in a bedroom, so that what Matthew 8:20 says might be verified: "Foxes have their dens, and the birds of

heaven have their nests. But the Son of Man has nowhere to rest his head." In a manger Christ is laid, so that what John 6:41 says might be demonstrated: "I am the living bread that has come down from heaven. . . ."[20]

Bonaventure concludes his extensive exposition of Luke 2:7 with these words:

> Therefore, the poor mother gave birth to the poor Christ in such a way that he might invite us to embrace poverty and to be enriched by his penury, according to what 2 Corinthians 8:9 says: "You know the graciousness of our Lord Jesus Christ, who, although he was rich, became poor for your sakes." And by means of his all-embracing indigence he condemned avaricious opulence. . . .From this it becomes clear to us that Jesus was really the Savior of the world, who from the first moment of his birth gave an example of virtue and shows the way of salvation. For in possessing a vile, humble, and poor bed, he already began to say that the world is to be despised with respect to the three things in it. Already by example he began to demonstrate the state of perfection which consists of humility, austerity, and poverty. Also in this the Lord manifests the disposition of highest condescension, because not only did he become a little child for us, but also became poor and despised for us, so that he could truly say what the Psalm has: "I am poor and in labors from my youth" (Ps 87:15).[21]

I contrast Bonaventure's emphasis on the humble and poor Jesus with that of Brendan Byrne who comments: "The visitor from God, who could not find hospitality in his own city, will nonetheless institute in the world the hospitality of God. The poor, marginalized shepherds of Bethlehem will be the first to experience it."[22]

Luke 6:20, the Primary Beatitude: Blessed are you poor,
for yours is the kingdom of God

Bonaventure's commentary is succinct and calls Jesus, "the Poor One":

> And note that Christ uses the present tense, "yours is," either on account of the certitude of the promise or even because truly poor persons are beginning now in some way to be kings, in accord with what 2 Corinthians 6:10 has: "as having nothing, yet possessing all things." And as it is said in 2 Corinthians 8:2:

"For their most profound poverty has abounded in the riches of generosity." So they are already quasi happy and not miserable like those poor who profess evangelical or voluntary poverty. . . .And note that Christ begins with poverty, for, as Ambrose says, "Poverty is the primal parent of the virtues, because the person who has despised secular things will merit eternal" and is a zealous follower of that Poor One, "who, although he was rich, became poor for our sakes," according to 2 Corinthians 8:9.[23]

Byrne deals with the contemporary issue of who constitute "the poor" and concludes: "In this perspective 'the poor' can include the afflicted in general, whatever the cause or nature of the affliction they suffer. 'The poor' are all whose emptiness and destruction provide scope for the generosity of God."[24]

Luke 7:22: The Poor have the gospel preached to them

Bonaventure's exegesis sings the praises of Jesus and of poverty as the foundation of evangelical perfection:

And that was a great prodigy that the names of the poor would become honorable and lovable and praiseworthy. And this occurred only because of Jesus, who made himself poor in order to enrich and honor us poor. 2 Corinthians 8:9 says: "You know the graciousness of our Lord Jesus Christ, for, although he was rich, he became poor for your sakes." And note that the text says, *The poor have the gospel preached to them,* rather than to those who are virgins or to those who are obedient. For poverty is the foundation of evangelical perfection. For just as avarice is the foundation of the city of Babylon, according to what 1 Timothy 6:10 has: "the root of all evil is avarice," and "pride is the beginning of every sin," according to Sirach 10:15, so poverty of spirit, which as poverty and humility includes the opposite of both aforementioned sins, is the foundation of evangelical perfection.[25]

Byrne notes that Luke 7:22 is a fulfillment of Isaiah 35:5 and 61:1, but makes no specific comment about "the poor have the good news preached to them."[26]

Luke 9:58: "The foxes have dens, and the birds of the air have nests, but the Son of Man has nowhere to lay his head."

In commenting on this verse, Bonaventure brings in begging:

> And therefore, an example of such imitation of the Lord is the mendicant, according to what 2 Corinthians 8:9 has: "He became poor for our sakes, so that by his poverty we might become rich." Wherefore, the imitators of Christ have been made rich by Christ's poverty. For exceedingly rich is the person who only has as much as the King of heaven and earth. Now a person of this type is the one who has nothing in property, but possesses everything in charity, like those in 2 Corinthians 6:10: "as having nothing, but possessing all things." Blessed are those who turn earthly dens into heavenly palaces.[27]

Byrne's comments are precise and not detailed: Following Jesus means a life of wandering with no guaranteed lodging.[28]

Luke 11:37: Jesus, the beggar, accepts the hospitality of a Pharisee

Both Bonaventure and Byrne comment on Jesus' second meal with a Pharisee, but from different angles.[29] Bonaventure accentuates Jesus' neediness:

> To relieve his hunger Christ accepted alms, not only accepted, but also begged, even when he was still twelve years old, as Bernard says in a certain Sermon: "When Jesus was twelve years old," etc. Bernard asks: Who gave Jesus food during the three days and answers: "So that you might take on all the misfortunes of human life and might conform yourself to our poverty in everything, you were begging alms at the gates as one of a crowd of the poor. Who will allow me to share in those morsels you begged or to be fed with the leftovers of that divine food?" 2 Corinthians 8:9 reads: "He became poor for us," etc. The Glossa on that passage has: "Don't be ashamed in your mendicancy to approach him who became poor for us."[30]

Byrne accurately points out how Jesus turns the table on his host, for Jesus is a guest who brings discomfort to his host as he engages in a sustained prophetic critique of the Pharisees and then the lawyers.[31]

Luke 12:21: Who is rich towards God?

In his commentary on the frightful example of the rich man in Luke 12:16-21, Bonaventure comes to this conclusion:

Now hope makes us *rich as regards God*. We have this hope in
God, according to what 1 Peter 1:3-4 has: "He has begotten us
again . . . unto a living hope, unto an incorruptible inheritance
. . . reserved in heaven." Now this type of hope is rooted in
poverty. So 2 Corinthians 6:10 states: "As poor, yet enriching
many; as having nothing, but possessing all things." Such a
person was Paul. Thus, he writes in Philippians 4:18: "I have all
and more than enough." Christ has made us such. Therefore, 2
Corinthians 8:9 says: "He became poor for your sakes, that by
his poverty you might become rich." Wherefore, he says to such
people: "Blessed are the poor in spirit, for theirs is the kingdom
of the heavens" (Matthew 5:3).[32]

Byrne doesn't explain the meaning of being "rich towards God,"
but does comment about greed:

> . . . nothing is more destructive of life and humanity than pre-
> occupation with acquiring, holding on to and increasing wealth.
> The problem is not so much the possession of riches as such. . . .
> Attachment to wealth is incompatible with living, sharing and
> celebrating the hospitality of God."[33]

Luke 14:1-24: Jesus is again at table with the Pharisees

Brendan Byrne is quick to observe that the invitation from a leading
Pharisee for Jesus to dine with him on a Sabbath "sets up an occasion
for conflict and instruction in the context of hospitality."[34] As in the ban-
quet portrayed in Luke 11:37-54, Jesus is a "disturbing guest."[35]

As we have come to expect, Bonaventure's interpretation moves in
another direction:

> In this action Christ's wonderful kindness is manifest. It is great
> in that he was associating with mortal human beings, although
> he was God. . . .Indeed, it was greater in that he was associating
> with his persecutors. . . .But his kindness is greatest, because
> his association took the form of intimate sharing of food, so
> that Revelation 3:20 may be fulfilled: "I stand at the door and
> knock. If anyone . . . opens the door for me, I will come in to
> him and will sup with him, and he with me." So through the
> fact that he entered a strange house, Christ's humility is com-
> mended. Through the fact that he entered a Pharisee's house,
> love. Through the fact that he ate a stranger's food, the poverty
> of Christ himself. And in these is shown the highest kindness,

by which the most high wanted to be humbled for us, the most just to associate with the impious, the most rich to become poor among men and women. Wherefore, 2 Corinthians 8:9 says: "You know the graciousness of our Lord Jesus Christ, that, although he was rich, he became poor for our sakes, so that by his poverty we might become rich."[36]

Luke 16:3: To dig I am unable, to beg I am ashamed

Those readers who have been paying close attention to Bonaventure's exegetical thought patterns know already how he is going to interpret this passage. Bonaventure observes:

But although these things (labor and shame) are difficult for the weak human being, they are, nevertheless, easy for the Christian made perfect by Christ. For Christ became poor for our sake and was in many labors, in accordance with the Psalm: "I am poor and in labors from my youth" (87:16). He makes labor palatable and begging honorable, for "it is a great honor to follow the Lord," as it is said in Sirach 23:38. Now the Lord himself says this about himself: "But I am a beggar and poor, and the Lord is solicitous for my welfare" (Psalm 39:18). Now this is not said with regard to spiritual things, in which the Lord abounds, but relative to temporal things. In these he became needy and a beggar for our sakes, according to what 2 Corinthians 8:9 states: "You know the graciousness of our Lord Jesus Christ, that, although he was rich, he became poor for our sakes," etc. And therefore, blessed Francis says in his Rule that his brothers "must not be ashamed of begging, because the Lord made himself poor in this world for our sakes." Nevertheless, the grace, which would have made the steward perfectly conformable to Christ, had not been given to him. So as an imperfect individual, he gives voice to his weakness: *I am ashamed to beg.*[37]

Byrne has no specific comment on Luke 16:3.[38]

Luke 21:4: The generous widow as an evangelical woman

The widow who put into the temple treasury all she had to live on is an imitator of Christ. As Bonaventure notes:

And thus she fulfilled the counsel, because she kept back nothing for herself, but gave everything. Thus she was beginning to be an evangelical woman, fulfilling the counsel of the Lord found in Luke 18:11 above: "If you wish to be perfect, go and sell all you have."

Bonaventure realizes that the widow can be criticized because she violated the virtuous middle road and observes:

> So she is praised by the divine mouth, because she placed her hope in Christ and fulfilled the divine counsel and chose the worship of God over her own personal need. Although this almsgiving did not seem to be prudent from a human standpoint, nonetheless she was most prudent since by giving all she had she became an imitator of Christ, about whom 2 Corinthians 8:9 says: "You know the graciousness of our Lord Jesus Christ—that although he was rich, he became poor for your sakes, so that by his poverty you might become rich.". . . When he (Christ) is the one giving the example, the middle ground is not abandoned, for he himself is the center of all perfection.[39]

Although he opts for another interpretation, Byrne considers the following interpretation valid: "Her offering of all she has to live on would represent a final instance in Luke's Gospel of the poor and marginalized demonstrating a devotion to God that shows up the failings of others."[40]

Part II

Bonaventure's View of the Evangelical Life

Space considerations prevent me from delving into every aspect of Bonaventure's view of evangelical life in Luke's Gospel.[41] For my purposes I concentrate on what Bonaventure has to say about the Lukan theme of "rich and poor."[42] In true Bonaventurian style I make three observations.

Distinction between the Avaricious and the Poor

First, unlike contemporary scholars, Bonaventure doesn't try to ascertain the social and economic circumstances behind Jesus' life and teaching. He is not a redaction critic interested in investigating what was going on in Luke's community. Although Bonaventure is acutely aware of Luke's literary style, he knows nothing of the implied or ideal reader of one style of contemporary literary criticism. For Bonaventure, love of money, whether this is called cupidity or avarice, is the determinant factor relative to possessions. So for Bonaventure the dichotomy is not "rich and poor," but "avaricious and poor" or better "lovers of money and poor disdainers of money."

Condemnation of Avarice

With this formulation of the dichotomy we are already at my second point, which is that Bonaventure does not condemn possessions, wealth, or rich people as such. What he condemns is avarice. I quote a long section from his *Commentary on the Gospel of Luke*, 18:24: "With what difficulty will they who have riches enter the kingdom of God." He writes, quoting the tradition formulated by Pseudo-Bernard, the *Glossa Interlinearis* and Bede:

> Bernard states: "Desire for the world is more harmful than the world's actual reality. And the principal reason why people should flee from riches is that they can scarcely or never be possessed without falling in love with them. For the actual reality of this world is slimy and sticky, and the human heart readily attaches itself to all the things whose company it keeps." And so the Glossa notes: "It is with difficulty that riches are contemned. Therefore, the safest policy by far is neither to possess nor fall in love with riches." From this one is given to understand that there are four different types of people set forth in Bede's interpretation and found in the Glossa on Mark 10:24: "Many have possessions and are not in love with them. Many do not have possessions and are in love with them. Some have possessions and are in love with them. Others rejoice that they neither have nor are in love with possessions. And these are the most secure people, for they can say with the Apostle: *The world has been crucified to me, and I to the world*, Galatians 6:14."[43]

Gospel Characters as Moral Examples

As one reads through Bonaventure's massive *Commentary on the Gospel of Luke*, it becomes clear that he is presenting individuals in the narrative as positive and negative examples to be followed.[44] My readers will not be surprised to see that the positive examples deal with poverty and humility, and the negative examples deal with avarice and arrogance.[45]

Positive Examples

Of course, the main positive example of the eight I mention is Jesus Christ, Son of God, Son of Mary.[46] In Part I above, I provided my readers with multiple instances of Jesus' being proposed as an example of generous poverty in accordance with 2 Corinthians 8:9. I repeat some here and add some more:

- Relative to Jesus' birth, Bonaventure comments: "And by means of his all-embracing indigence he condemned avaricious opulence."[47]
- Bonaventure uses the story of Jesus' cure of a man's withered hand to make the point that avarice dries out the soul whereas almsgiving preserves it. He writes of Luke 6:11: "Moreover, the sick man with a dried up hand signifies the dryness of avarice, which is cured, when by divine command the hand is extended to grant alms, according to what Proverbs 31:20 says: 'She has opened her hand to the needy and stretched out her hands to the poor.'"[48]
- Bonaventure observes about Luke 9:57, which depicts Jesus' journey with his disciples: ". . . the disciples were walking with the Lord on the way of perfection. . . ."[49] When someone tries to join Jesus and his disciples on their journey, Jesus replies in Luke 9:58 about foxes having dens and the birds of the air having nests, but the Son of Man having nowhere to lay his head. Bonaventure explains: "In this he shows wondrous poverty, as if he were saying that the person who loves earthly things will not have him as a companion. Therefore, Luke 14:33 below says: 'Whoever has not renounced all that he possesses cannot be my disciple,' that is, a perfect imitator."[50]
- As you may well recall, Bonaventure interprets Jesus' second meal with a Pharisee as an instance of Jesus begging for his sustenance.[51]
- In his conversation with the very rich ruler, Jesus comes to the point in Luke 18:22 of inviting him to follow him: "One thing is still lacking to you. Sell all that you have and give to the poor, and you will have treasure in heaven. And come, follow me." Bonaventure's exposition is pointed: "And Luke 6:40 above reads: 'But when perfected, everyone will be like his teacher, that is, Christ who had absolutely nothing.'"[52]
- The supreme example of Christ's poverty takes place at his crucifixion. Already in his introduction to Jesus' third prediction of his passion (Luke 18:31-34), Bonaventure notes: ". . . here . . . he shows

that it [poverty] is to be approved and chosen by reason of the most perfect example, namely, Christ crucified."[53] I quote three passages from Bonaventure's exposition of Christ's crucifixion. In interpreting Luke 23:33 he observes: "Now the cross, by which the world is crucified, is poverty of spirit, which has four arms, that is, contempt of glory, money, nation and family."[54] In commenting on Luke 23:34, Bonaventure contrasts the nakedness of Christ with the greediness of the soldiers who take his clothes. He writes: "For David says in the Psalm: 'They divided my garments among them, and for my vesture they cast lots' (Ps 21:19). And in this is manifest the rapacity of the soldiers, who stripped Christ naked out of their greediness."[55] For his postill on Luke 23:37, Bonaventure is indebted to Bernard of Clairvaux: "'. . .Now by these gems of the virtues the four corners of the cross are adorned: love at the top; obedience on the right; patience on the left; and the root of virtues, humility, at the base. The consummation of the Lord's passion has enriched the triumphant trophy of the cross with these virtues.'"[56] It seems clear that "poverty of spirit" and "humility" are variants of Bonaventure's more dominant viewpoint: no love of money, no avarice, no cupidity.

- Jesus' mother is poor. I remind you of Bonaventure's comments: "Therefore, the poor mother gives birth to the poor Christ in such a way that he might invite us to embrace poverty and to be enriched by his penury, according to what 2 Corinthians 8:9 says. . . ."[57]

- John the Baptist manifests a life of poverty in his food and vesture, as Bonaventure comments on Luke 7:25: "He was truly one of those evangelical men about whom it is said in 1 Timothy 6:8: 'Having food and wherewith to be covered, with these let us be content.'"[58]

- Besides being an example of the active life, Martha is also an example of taking care of the needy. Bonaventure comments on Luke 10:38: *"And a certain woman, named Martha, welcomed him into her house*, namely, as someone poor and needy. Wherefore, to such people he will say in the judgment what Matthew 25:35 has: 'I was a stranger, and you took me in,' that is, to those similar to Martha who is like Job, of whom Job 31:32 says: 'The stranger did not stay outside my door. My door was open to the traveler.'"[59]

- Bonaventure has much to say about the positive apostolic example of Peter: "So first, concerning poverty's authentication by apostolic observance the text has: *But Peter said: Behold, we have left all and have followed you.* Peter says this as the prince of the apostles, upon whom ecclesiastical perfection has been built. . . .He also says this to show that the Apostles had fulfilled the counsel of poverty. . . .So since all things could be desired, they left all things when they left their desires behind. Peter also says this not in a boastful way to draw attention to himself, but in the manner of a sage who invites others to imitation."[60]

- It is not surprising that Zacchaeus, whose story occurs immediately after Jesus' gift of sight to the blind beggar, is hailed by Bonaventure as a model of one seeking wisdom and of liberality. Bonaventure notes: "So this man was already fulfilling the counsel of the Sage according to Proverbs 8:10: 'Receive my instruction, and not money. Choose knowledge rather than gold.'"[61]

- We have already been treated to Bonaventure's interpretation of the poor widow in Luke 21:1-4. This generous widow is an evangelical woman, for she fulfills the command to the perfect, that is, she abandons all and thus imitates Christ, who gave away all that he had.[62]

- For Bonaventure Luke's final teaching about the evil of avarice is found in the person of Joseph of Arimathea. In his postill on Luke 23:50, Bonaventure maintains that Joseph is a decurion and therefore has the qualities of Moses' assistants according to Exodus 18:21-22, that is, there is no avarice in him.[63]

Negative Examples

Some of ten negative examples that I highlight from Bonaventure's Commentary may surprise us, e.g., the blind man as a sign of avarice.

- In one of his spiritual interpretations of Luke 6:6-11, Bonaventure says that the sick man with a dried up hand signifies the dryness of avarice and that it is cured when the hand is extended to grant alms, according to what Proverbs 31:20 says: "She has opened her hand to the needy and stretched out her hands to the poor."[64]

- In his commentary on Luke 12:15, Bonaventure says of the rich fool that avarice blinded him.[65]

- The woman who had been bent over for eighteen years is a sign of avarice. Bonaventure's observations on Luke 13:11 include this spiritual interpretation: "Now this long-lived curvature can be understood as the sickness of avarice and cupidity, which inclines the heart to temporal things. The Psalm has: 'They have set their eyes bowing down to the earth' (Ps 16:11). This infirmity of being bowed down had lasted for eighteen years, that is, throughout the entirety of life. For as Jerome says: 'While all other vices become decrepit in old people, only avarice is ever young.'"[66]

- Bonaventure is right at home with some contemporary commentators who maintain that dropsy in Luke signifies avarice.[67] His exposition of Luke 14:6 reads: "First is the illness of dropsy, whose characteristic feature, as the *Glossa* says, is that 'the more one drinks, the more thirsty one becomes.' And in this it designates every concupiscence, which can never be satiated, and especially avarice, according to what Proverbs 30:16 says: 'Fire never says: It is enough.'"[68]

- The Pharisees are a negative example of avarice, as Bonaventure observes on Luke 16:14: "Therefore, the *Glossa* comments: 'They deride him, the teacher of mercy and humility and frugality, as if he were commanding harmful things, things less than beneficial and never to be done.'[69] And like the avaricious, they mock his praises of largess."

- Another negative example is the rich man who neglected Lazarus the poor beggar. In his commentary on Luke 16:19, Bonaventure observes: "First, then, concerning the lust of the eyes the text says: *'There was a certain rich man.'* This man is said to be rich, not only on account of his possession of riches, but also because of his love of them. For which reason 1 Timothy 6:9 reads: 'Those who seek to become rich fall into temptation and the snare of the devil,' etc. For through its love for earthly things the spirit grows fat and is weighed down, so that it cannot travel into the higher realms of heaven."[70]

- The very rich ruler of Luke 18:18-30, another negative example, is mortified to hear Jesus tell him to give away his possessions. Bonaventure has this to say about the ruler's response to Jesus' invitation to follow him: "For since he abounded in riches, he abhorred the penury of poverty, and therefore, he was rendered sad when Christ praised and counseled poverty. And this is the consequence of cupidity and an indication of grasping after possessions that a person is saddened by the horror of poverty."[71]

- Luke places Jesus' giving sight to a blind man (18:35-43) right after Jesus' call of the very rich ruler and the third prediction of his passion. Bonaventure is quick to see similarities and note contrasts. He writes: "And this blind person represents the human race, which is blind on account of the lack of the light of wisdom and mendicant on account of a defect in grace and justice. . . .Now the human race has been blinded by cupidity towards temporal things. . . .Human beings, by falling in love with things, are blinded and rendered foolish."[72] Bonaventure interprets the blind beggar's insistence that Jesus, Son of David, grant him his sight in this wise: "The *Glossa* notes: 'The blind man does not ask for gold or any temporal thing, but only for light. Therefore, let us imitate in body and mind the person we have heard had been cured.'"[73]

- Jesus' cleansing of the temple also speaks against avarice. As Bonaventure says about Luke 19:45: "Now the fact that the Lord cast out the buyers and the sellers shows that he especially condemns avarice among the clergy and simony above all."[74]
- Finally, it is "the thirst of avarice" that motivates Judas to betray Jesus.[75]

In conclusion, readers can hardly listen to a single chapter of Bonaventure's *Commentary on the Gospel of Luke* without hearing the drumbeat of "voluntary poverty is good" and "avarice is evil." Not only is this drumbeat constant, but it is also reinforced by the words and actions of the characters of the Gospel, who in positive and negative ways dramatize Bonaventure's point. As we hear the drumbeat and are caught up in the story by its characters, we might well wonder what prompted Bonaventure to write his *Commentary* in such a fashion. In the third and final part I give some hints on what may be behind Bonaventure's *Commentary*.

Part III

What prompted St. Bonaventure to Emphasize Certain Parts of Luke's Teaching about Christ and the Evangelical Life?

This section will have two components. First, I look at Bonaventure's Commentary on Luke's Gospel as a window and then examine it as a mirror.

The Commentary on Luke's Gospel as a Window

In the case of Brendan Byrne, it is easy to ascertain why he emphasized certain parts of Luke's teaching about Christ and the spiritual life, for he tells us. He is writing from a personal point of view, one that he finds attractive and helpful in making the Gospel of Luke speak to contemporary people. While he acknowledges that his reading is not the only possible reading of Luke, he believes that his reading is valid and firmly rooted in the actual text of Luke's Gospel. While he is aware of feminist and liberation readings and also of the way the Gospel text may be open to anti-Jewish readings, he does not devote great space to these concerns. In brief, his "interpretation of Luke stems from a faith commitment and a conviction that the Gospel's essential purpose is to bring home to people a sense of the extravagance of God's love in their regard."[76]

Alas and alack, Bonaventure has not told us what is behind the writing of his *Commentary on the Gospel of Luke*. Of course, his massive Commentary is explicable at one level as something he had to do on the way to obtaining his "doctorate." On another level it is something that he revised extensively for preachers. In this form it may date to the time when Bonaventure was General Minister of the Order of Friars Minor and had the assistance of many professional scribes, say, 1265.

But I would venture to say that, on a far deeper level, its origin lies in his Franciscan soul and the controversy over absolute poverty and the legitimacy of the Franciscan movement. He reveals his Franciscan soul, it seems to me, in the four times he refers to Blessed Francis of Assisi[77] and the one time he refers to Giles of Assisi, one of Francis's earliest companions.[78] While Francis surely is a positive example of missionary activity, daily cross bearing and begging in imitation of the Lord Jesus, and Giles is an illustrious example of contemplation, it seems extraordinary to mention these figures in a *Commentary* that might be meant only for the lecture hall. It seems to me that Bonaventure's Franciscan heart is evident in his mention of these Franciscan luminaries.

But in my mind, the greatest putative background for his *Commentary on the Gospel of Luke* is his sometimes very heated discussions with secular masters over the nature of the evangelical life and absolute poverty and his dealings with the spiritual wing of the Friars Minor.[79] Here I limit myself to the issue of absolute poverty. Rather than rehearse this entire topic with its extensive bibliography,[80] I will consider the commonalities between Bonaventure's Commentary on Luke's Gospel and his *Quaestiones disputatae de perfectione evangelica (Disputed Questions on Evangelical Perfection)*,[81] written in 1255, and his *Apologia pauperum (Defense of the Mendicants)*, written in 1269.

Bonaventure's *Quaestiones disputatae de perfectione evangelica*

In treating Bonaventure's *Disputed Questions on Evangelical Perfection*, I will limit myself to Question II, which deals with poverty, and to article 1 of that question, which considers poverty from the viewpoint of renunciation.[82]

Since this is a *quaestio disputata*, to compare it with a commentary may be similar to comparing giants to angels. But there still may be some commonalities. Bonaventure marshals fifteen Scripture texts in his argument that it is the hallmark of Christian perfection to renounce everything, both in common and in private. Among these fifteen texts, we should not be surprised that four come from Luke's Gospel[83] and one is 2 Corinthians 8:9.[84] I skip over Bonaventure's eleven citations from "the witness of the Saints" and focus on the first argument of the seven that he provides from reason. It is the very familiar image of the two cities: Jerusalem and Babylon:

> There are two cities, namely, God's and the devil's, Jerusalem and Babylon. They are opposed to one another both in themselves and in their foundations. Now, as Augustine states, the foundation of the city of Babylon is cupidity. Therefore, the more a person moves away from cupidity the more that person moves away from the city of the devil. But poverty, through which a person totally renounces everything in common and in private, both through action and through affection, is that which moves the greatest distance away from avarice. Therefore, etc.[85]

We found something similar above in Bonaventure's exposition of Luke 7:22,[86] and we will find something equally similar in what Bonaventure says in his *Apologia pauperum*.

From this sampling of commonalities between Bonaventure's *Quaestiones disputatae de perfectione evangelica* and his *Commentary on the Gospel of Luke*, I would suggest that these questions are operative in the background of his *Commentary*.

Bonaventure's *Apologia pauperum*[87]

In my consideration of Bonaventure's *Apologia pauperum (Defense of the Mendicants)*, I will limit myself to chapter seven, which has abundant arguments from Scripture and bears the title: "First Point of the Third Answer, in which Voluntary and Strict Poverty are shown to be the Foundation of Evangelical Perfection, and possible Objections are answered."[88] While this work is obviously different in literary style and argument from his *Commentary on the Gospel of Luke*, it has sufficient commonalities to indicate that Bonaventure may have been following well-used thought patterns in each.[89]

In both works, Bonaventure stresses the example of the Lord Jesus. For instance, in the first two paragraphs of chapter seven, Bonaventure contrasts the foundation of the city of Babylon, which is covetousness, with the foundation of the New Jerusalem, which is Christ's poverty. Bonaventure writes: "Jesus Christ, the Origin of all good, the Foundation and Founder of the New Jerusalem who *appeared to this end, that he might destroy the works of the devil*, embraced with great eagerness the very opposite of such covetousness, advocating poverty by his example and preaching it by his word."[90] In his exegesis of Luke 7:22, that is, "the poor have the gospel preached to them," Bonaventure employs this same terminology and refers to avarice as the foundation of the city of Babylon.

Bonaventure devotes the entirety of paragraph 7 of the *Apologia* to the poverty of Jesus and his poor mother.[91] As we have seen, much of his commentary on Luke 2:7 (n. 11-16) spotlights the poor Mary and the poor Jesus.

Bonaventure devotes two extensive paragraphs in n. 21-22 of the *Apologia* to nakedness of the heart and body and concludes by quoting Jerome:

> "Do you wish to be perfect and to stand in the first rank of dignity? Do as the apostles did. Sell all you have, give to the poor, and follow the Savior, and in your destitution and solitude you will be following the naked and lonely cross." By these words he clearly asserts that this poverty reaches the summit of perfection, and that, through it, a man more expressly and closely embraces the nakedness of the cross and imitates the stripped Crucified.[92]

In his commentary on Luke 23:34 (n. 42), Bonaventure contrasts the greediness of the soldiers and Christ's nakedness.

In paragraph 9 of the *Apologia*, Bonaventure shows how the Lord Jesus set up absolute poverty as an example for the apostles to follow:

> And since it is for our sake, and not his own, that Christ the Master and Lord chose to assume poverty, showing us perfection through what he did, it follows that he set up absolute pov-

erty as an example to be imitated by the holy apostles, the perfect followers of his holiness, as shown in Matthew, Mark, and Luke."[93]

Besides the commonality of the example of Jesus, his Mother and his disciples, there is also the commonality of citing the same ecclesiastical authors. In paragraph 6 of the *Apologia,* Bonaventure cites Bernard's sermon, "When Jesus was twelve years old," in order to show that the poor Jesus begged for his sustenance.[94] This selfsame citation occurs in Bonaventure's commentary on Luke 11:37 (n. 78).

In paragraph 13 of the *Apologia*, Bonaventure cites Rabanus about the reactions of four different types of people in the face of possessions. In his commentary on Luke 18:24 (n. 43) Bonaventure quotes this same basic passage, but attributes it to Bede, as found in the *Glossa.* Significantly both citations conclude with Galatians 6:14.

Besides the commonalities of the same examples and the same ecclesiastical authors, there is also the commonality of the same citations from Sacred Writ. In the *Apologia,* Bonaventure refers three times to 2 Corinthians 8:9 (paragraphs 14, 15, 35).[95] While these citations may not have the same christological thrust as those in his *Commentary on the Gospel of Luke*, they still show what a key text this was for Bonaventure. While Bonaventure does make reference to the mission-sending passages of Luke 9:3 and 10:4 in paragraph 11 of the *Apologia*,[96] his primary concern is with parallel texts from Matthew, the ecclesiastical gospel. Thus, for example, Jesus' command to the young man, "If you will be perfect, go, sell what you have and give to the poor . . . and come, follow me," is quoted from Matthew 19:21 rather than from Luke 18:24.[97] Further, Bonaventure makes much of Matthew 10:9 ("Do not take gold and silver"),[98] Acts 3:6 ("Silver and gold I have none") in n. 12,[99] and the money bag of John 12:6 in n. 35-40.[100]

In summary, there seem to be sufficient commonalities in the examples, ecclesiastical authors and citations from Sacred Scripture to allow us to peer through the window of Bonaventure's *Commentary on the Gospel of Luke* to the heated discussions he was having with the university doctors, especially William of Saint-Amour and Gerard of Abbeville.

The *Commentary on the Gospel of Luke* as a Mirror

It is now time to zero in on Bonaventure's *Commentary* as a mirror. I will be short and leave to Franciscan preachers and formation directors the task of deepening the message of Luke and Bonaventure. It is always comforting to ask questions about what was going on behind the scenes of a text and thus view it as a window. But when we begin to treat Luke and Bonaventure as mirrors, especially on their theme of "rich and poor," then we are in for challenges aplenty.

Might our United States consumerist culture be afflicting us all with a case of moral dropsy? We have to have a bigger and better house, a slimmer and technologically richer cell phone, the latest TV, sound system and computer. And the academics among us have to purchase more and more books. Our society wants us to turn a deaf ear to Bonaventure's drumbeat of "Our Savior, the Lord Jesus, used his riches in generosity to others." Our society tells us to look abstractly at and don't get involved in Luke's and Bonaventure's positive and negative examples, lest they change our lives.

I invite you, at your leisure, to take a courageous and generous look into the mirror of Luke and Bonaventure. You might even want to engage a Franciscan preacher who will polish this mirror and hold it steady so that you can behold your life with all its beauty and blemishes.

Conclusion

How is one to judge Bonaventure's interpretation of the Christology of the Gospel of Luke? Both Luke and Bonaventure write from the perspective of faith, that is, neither writes to depict what actually happened in first-century Galilee. Bonaventure is prone to latch onto Luke's portrayal of Jesus as Son of God and Son of Mary. While Luke evidences some dependence upon wisdom traditions such as that behind Luke 10:21-25 and 11:31, it is Bonaventure who exploits these to their christological depth. Although there is some scholarly discussion of the interconnections between the Pastoral Epistles where 1 Timothy 2:5 occurs ("There is one mediator between God and humans, Jesus Christ"),[101] I know of no scholar who would maintain that Luke's Christology has as one of its ingredients Jesus as the Center. Finally, while I might be tempted to interpret Jesus' incarnation in Luke's Gospel via Paul's hymn of kenosis in Philippians 2:6-11, I would not have immediately interpreted it, as Bonaventure does, via 2 Corinthians 8:9.

As Bonaventure's frequent references to the Wisdom Literature and even to Seneca attest,[102] his contrast between the foundation of the New Jerusalem in the voluntary poverty of Jesus the Lord and the foundation of Babylon in avarice is heavily influenced by the teaching of the sages. But Bonaventure has gone beyond the sages by presenting concrete positive and negative examples, especially the positive example of the Lord Jesus Christ. While most contemporary Lukan scholars would not lay the emphasis on the theme of rich and poor in the same way that Bonaventure does, they would have to acknowledge that he is dealing with the text of Luke's Gospel and not smuggling in huge amounts of extraneous interpretive material.

Though I have tried to make the case that behind Bonaventure's exposition of Luke's Gospel stands the controversy over absolute poverty, I cannot demonstrate my contention. It seems highly unlikely that the controversy over this matter, which raged for some fifteen years, would not have left more than one mark on the *Commentary on the Gospel of Luke* that Bonaventure was working at, on and off, during the same time period.

Endnotes

[1]See *S. Bonaventurae Commentarius in Evangelium S. Lucae*, volume VII (Quaracchi: Collegium S. Bonaventurae, 1895), 3-604. See also *St. Bonaventure's Commentary on the Gospel of Luke: Chapters 1-8, 9-16, 17-24*, Bonaventure Texts in Translation Series, VIII/1-3, trans. Robert J. Karris (St. Bonaventure, NY: Franciscan Institute Publications, 2001, 2003, 2004). In what follows, these volumes of translation will be referred to by Roman numeral and page number. Thus, I, 666.

[2]See *S. Bonaventurae Commentaria in quatuor libros sententiarum Magistri Petri Lombardi*, Volume III (Quaracchi: Collegium S. Bonaventurae, 1887), 6-468.

[3]"For you know the graciousness of our Lord Jesus Christ: how, although he was rich, he became poor for your sakes, so that by his poverty you might become rich."

[4]Brendan Byrne, SJ, *The Hospitality of God: A Reading of Luke's Gospel* (Collegeville: Liturgical Press, 2000). I select Byrne's study because of its contemporary nature, conciseness and clarity. While it may not provide the scope of multi-volume commentaries on Luke, it is adequate for my purposes of comparison.

[5]It may not surprise us that while the reality of hospitality and the reality of poverty and humility are present in the texts that Byrne and Bonaventure investigate, the actual terminology is generally absent. For example, in Luke's birth scene there is no mention of God's hospitality in that Jesus came as a stranger and was offered no hospitality. Nor, for that matter, does Luke 2:1-7 explicitly say that Mary and Jesus were poor and humble.

[6]See his *The Gospel According to Luke (I-IX)*, Anchor Bible, 28 (Garden City, NY: Doubleday, 1981), 192-218.

[7]Luke 5:28 (n. 71) in I, 439-40.

[8]Luke 20:44 (n. 50-51) in III, 1948-50.

[9]Luke 11:31 (n. 67) in II, 1092.

[10]Luke 11:32 (n. 68) in II, 1093. For a more complete treatment of Bonaventure's anti-Judaism, see II, xiii-lvi.

[11]*The Hidden Center: Spirituality and Speculative Christology in St. Bonaventure*, Franciscan Pathways (St. Bonaventure, NY: Franciscan Institute, 2000). See also Zachary Hayes, "The

Life and Christological Thought of St. Bonaventure," in *Franciscan Christology: Selected Texts, Translations and Introductory Essays*, ed. Damian McElrath (St. Bonaventure, NY: The Franciscan Institute, 1994), 59-88.

[12]Luke 4:30 (n. 61) in I, 343-44. See also Bonaventure's commentary on Luke 4:18 (n. 36) in I, 320: "First, then, it is indicated that he is mediator through the mystery of the incarnation when it says: *The Spirit of the Lord is upon me, because he has anointed me. Me* points here to the person of Christ in his assumed nature, upon which the Holy Spirit has come to rest, according to what Isaiah 11:2 says: 'And the Spirit of the Lord will rest upon him.'"

[13]*The Hidden Center*, 63.

[14]See Luke 24:36 (n. 36) in III, 2229.

[15]See Luke 11:31 (n. 66) in II, 1091.

[16]See Luke 11:31 (n. 66) in II, 1091-92, n. 198, for greater detail on John 8:25, which Bonaventure cites five times. See his comments on Luke: 7:14 (n. 25); 8:15 (n. 22); 9:35 (n. 65); 11:31 (n. 66); 22:44 (n. 51).

[17]See Luke 11:31 (n. 67) in II, 1092.

[18]See III, pp. 2415-16 for the ten references. The passage Bonaventure cites most frequently (14 times) is Revelations 3:20: "Behold, I stand at the door and knock. If any person listens to my voice and opens the door to me, I will come in to him and will dine with him, and he with me." See III, 2426.

[19]See Luke 2:7 (n. 11) in I, 145. Bonaventure cites 1 Timothy 6:7-10 some 18 times.

[20]See Luke 2:7 (n. 12) in I, 146).

[21]See Luke 2:7 (n. 15-16) in I, 150-52.

[22]*Hospitality of God*, 32.

[23]See Luke 6:20 (n. 51) in I, 503-505.

[24]*Hospitality of God*, 66.

[25]See Luke 7:22 (n. 40-41) in I, 603. Bonaventure goes on to glorify the ten characteristics of poverty. See Luke 7:22 (n. 42-43) in I, 604-605 and Robert J. Karris, "St. Bonaventure as Biblical Interpreter: His Methods, Wit, and Wisdom," *Franciscan Studies* 60 (2002): 159-208 (here 198-202).

[26]*Hospitality of God*, 71.

[27]See Luke 9:58 (n. 105) in II, 912-13.

[28]*Hospitality of God*, 94.

[29]See Luke 7:36-50 for the first meal and Luke 14:1-24 for the third.

[30]See Luke 11:37 (n. 78) in II, 1103-04.

[31]*Hospitality of God*, 112.

[32]See Luke 12:21 (n. 31) in II, 1165.

[33]*Hospitality of God*, 115.

[34]*Hospitality of God*, 122.

[35]*Hospitality of God*, 123.

[36]See Luke 14:1 (n. 2) in II, 1318-19.

[37]See Luke 16:3 (n. 6) in III, 1478-79.

[38]See *Hospitality of God*, 134.

[39]See Luke 21:4 (n. 5-6) in III, 1964-1965.

[40]*Hospitality of God*, 160.

[41]I recommend two studies on Luke's view of the spiritual life: Brian E. Beck, *Christian Character in the Gospel of Luke* (London: Epworth, 1989) and James L. Resseguie, *Spiritual Landscape: Images of the Spiritual Life in the Gospel of Luke* (Peabody, MA: Hendricksons, 2004). See also Robert J. Karris, *Prayer and the New Testament: Jesus and His Communities at Worship* (New York: Crossroad, 2000), 40-81.

[42]See Beck, *Christian Character*, 28-54, 190-94 and Resseguie, *Spiritual Landscape*, 101-14, 155-61 for their assessment of how possessions tie in with the spiritual life. For an

overview of the thematic of "rich and poor" in the scholarly literature, see Thomas E. Phillips, "Reading Recent Readings of Issues of Wealth and Poverty in Luke and Acts," *Currents in Biblical Research* 1.2 (2003): 231-69.

[43]See Luke 18:24 (n. 43) in III, 1759-60. For a behind-the-scenes view of poverty in thirteenth-century Paris, see Sharon Farmer, *Surviving Poverty in Medieval Paris: Gender, Ideology, and the Daily Lives of the Poor* (Ithaca, NY: Cornell University Press, 2002). Among other things, Farmer notes that of the 200,000 people who lived in Paris in the thirteenth century, some ten percent were beggars and that only twenty-five percent of the population earned enough money to pay taxes. Bonaventure would consider most of these poor people to belong to the category of the involuntary poor.

[44]Bonaventure gives an explanation of this in his exposition of Luke 16:8 (n. 12) in II, 1485-86.

[45]The list of moral examples I give is not exhaustive.

[46]See *Apologia pauperum*, chapter 2, n. 13, in Omnia Opera 8.243, for the six ways in which Bonaventure categorizes Jesus' actions in an attempt to show which actions are imitable.

[47]See Luke 2:7 (n. 15) in I, 150-51.

[48]See Luke 6:11 (n. 23) in I, 475.

[49]See Luke 9:57 (n. 103) in II, 910.

[50]See Luke 9:58 (n. 104) in II, 911.

[51]See Luke 11:37 (n. 78), in II, 1103-04.

[52]See Luke 18:22 (n. 41) in III, 1754.

[53]See Luke 18:30 (n. 52) in III, 1772.

[54]See Luke 23:33 (n. 40) in III, 2151.

[55]See Luke 23:34 (n. 42) in III, 2153.

[56]See Luke 23:37 (n. 45) in III, 2158.

[57]See Luke 2:7 (n. 15) in I, 150.

[58]See Luke 7:25 (n. 49) in I, 611.

[59]See Luke 10:38 (n. 38) in II, 994.

[60]See Luke 18:28 (n. 47) in III, 1764-65.

[61]See Luke 19:3 (n. 4) in III, 1792.

[62]See Luke 21:1-4 (n. 1-6) in III,1959-66.

[63]See Luke 23:50 (n. 60) in III, 2174.

[64]See Luke 6:11 (n. 23) in I, 475.

[65]See Luke 12:15 n. 24-25 in II, 1157-59.

[66]See Luke 13:11 (n. 24) in II, 1255. It should be remembered that Bonaventure's dominant interpretive paradigm is not history. Thus, he is not putting down this ailing woman who has suffered so much for so long a time, but is interpreting her plight spiritually, as a type. Bonaventure's interpretation of this woman's illness is similar to his exposition of the man with the withered hand in Luke 6:6-11.

[67]See, e.g., Willi Braun, *Feasting and Social Rhetoric in Luke 14*, Society for New Testament Studies, Monograph Series 85 (Cambridge: Cambridge University Press, 1995), 22-42.

[68]See Luke 14:6 (n. 11) in II, 1324.

[69]See Luke 16:14 (n. 26) in II, 1503.

[70]See Luke 16:19 (n. 36) in II, 1517.

[71]See Luke 18:23 (n. 42) in III, 1756.

[72]See Luke 18:35 (n. 35) in III, 1780-81.

[73]See Luke 18:40-41 (n. 64) in III, 1786.

[74]See Luke 20:45 (n. 70) in III, 1884.

[75]See Luke 22:4 (n. 5) in III, 2032.

[76]*Hospitality of God*, 3; also 2-4.

[77]See Luke 9:3 (n. 5) in II, 803: "So also Blessed Francis, when he used to send the brothers out to preach, used to say to them the words of the Psalm: 'Cast your care upon the Lord,' etc. (54:23)." See also Luke 9:3 (n. 7) in II, 805-806, about the bare essentials of clothing: "Similarly Blessed Francis avoided such duplicity, for when he was ill, he refused to have a piece of fur put on his chest inside his habit if a piece of fur would not also be placed on the outside of his habit." See further Luke 9:23 (n. 38) in II, 838, about daily cross bearing: "Note that he says: *daily*, because daily the penitence of the cross must be new and fresh, so that he may always say: 'I said: Now I have begun' (Psalm 76:11) like Blessed Francis, who, when he was dying, said that now he was beginning to do good: 'Brothers, let us begin and make progress, for up unto now we have made little progress.'" Finally, see Luke 16:3 (n. 6) in II, 1478, where Bonaventure couples Christ, the beggar, with Francis and his Rule about begging: "In these he (the Lord) became needy and a beggar for our sakes, according to what 2 Corinthians 8:9 states. . . . And therefore, Blessed Francis says in his Rule that his brothers 'must not be ashamed of begging, because the Lord made himself poor in this world for our sakes.'"

[78]See Luke 9:28 (n. 48) in II, 850-51, and Blessed Giles's seven steps of contemplation: "There are seven steps of contemplation. The first is fire, the second is anointing, the third is ecstasy, the fourth is contemplation, the fifth is enjoyment, the sixth is rest, the seventh is glory."

[79]Cf. Sean Kinsella, "The Poverty of Christ in the Medieval Debates between the Papacy and the Franciscans," *Laurentianum* 36 (1995): 477-509. This source is especially good on Bonaventure's concern for and with the Spirituals.

[80]For general background see D. L. Douie, *The Conflict Between the Seculars and the Mendicants at the University of Paris in the Thirteenth Century*, The Aquinas Society of London, Aquinas Paper No. 23 (London: Blackfriars, 1954); Decima L. Douie, "St Bonaventura's Part in the Conflict between Seculars and Mendicants at Paris," in *S. Bonaventura 1274-1974*, Volume II, ed. Jacques Guy Bougerol (Grottaferrata: Collegio S. Bonaventura, 1973), 585-612; Roberto Lambertini, *Apologia e crescita dell' identità francescana (1255-1279)*, Istituto storico italiano per il Medio Evo, Nuovi studi storici 4 (Rome: Nella sede dell'istituto, 1990); Malcolm D. Lambert, *Franciscan Poverty: The Doctrine of the Absolute Poverty of Christ and the Apostles in the Franciscan Order 1210-1323*, revised and expanded edition (St. Bonaventure, NY: The Franciscan Institute, 1998), esp. 133-48; Kinsella, "The Poverty of Christ," 477-509; Roberto Lambertini, *La povertà pensata: Evoluzione storica della definizione dell'identità minoritica da Bonaventura ad Ockham*, Collana di storia medievale 1 (Modena: Mucchi, 2000), esp. 29-79; Andrew Traver, *The Opuscula of William of Saint-Amour: The Minor Works of 1255-1256*, Beiträge zur Geschichte der Philosophie und Theologie des Mittelalters, NF 63 (Münster: Aschendorff, 2003).

[81]See *Omnia Opera* 5:117-98.

[82]See *Omnia Opera* 5:124-134.

[83]Luke 12:24 in n. 5 in 5:125; Luke 14:33 in n. 6 in 5:125; Luke 9:58 in n. 9 in 5:125; Luke 2:7 in n. 13 in 5:126. Since Bonaventure cites the Matthean version (Matt. 19:21 and 19:27) of Jesus' invitation to the young man and Peter's response rather than the parallel in Luke 18:22 and 18:28, I cannot add n. 1 and 2 in 5:125 to my list of times that Bonaventure cites Luke.

[84]See n. 11 in 5:126.

[85]See n. 26 in 5:127.

[86]See Luke 7:22 (n. 40-41) in I, 603.

[87]See *Omnia Opera* 8:233-330. Subsequent citations will eliminate *Omnia Opera*.

[88]See 8:272-86, esp. 272. See *Defense of the Mendicants*, trans. José de Vinck, Bonaventure Texts in Translation Series (Paterson, NJ: St. Anthony Guild Press, 1965), 125-63, 301-304. I have occasionally modified de Vinck's translation.

[89]The parallels may well be indicative only, for besides Luke's Gospel Bonaventure also deals extensively with Matthew 10:9 ("Do not take gold and silver"), Acts 3:6 ("I have neither silver nor gold") and John 12:6 (Judas is in control of the money bag), and quotes many ecclesiastical writers that he did not cite in his Commentary on the Gospel of Luke.

[90]See 8:272 and *Defense of the Mendicants*, 126.

[91]See 8:274.

[92]See 8:279-280 and *Defense of the Mendicants*, 147-48.

[93]See *Defense of the Mendicants*, 133. See n. 11 on 135-36, where Bonaventure treats Luke 9:3 and 10:4.

[94]See 8:274.

[95]See 8:276-77, 284.

[96]See 8:275-76.

[97]See n. 13 in 8:276.

[98]See n. 5-6, 11 in 8:273-74, 275.

[99]See 8:276.

[100]See 8:284-86.

[101]See, e.g., Stephen G. Wilson, *Luke and the Pastoral Epistles* (London: SPCK, 1979).

[102]See the cumulative index in III, 2459 ff. Bonaventure cites Seneca more than ten times, especially in contexts of being content with little.

CHAPTER FOUR

OLD TESTAMENT WISDOM LITERATURE, CREATION AND ST. FRANCIS OF ASSISI

Michael D. Guinan, O.F.M.

I taught my first course in Old Testament Wisdom Literature over thirty years ago, and it already felt like familiar territory. Over the years, as my knowledge of both Wisdom Literature and the Franciscan tradition expanded, the fit between these two areas only deepened. Trying to articulate exactly how and why proved a bit more elusive. In what follows, I would like to address this issue more reflectively through five steps: Wisdom Literature, Wisdom Quotations, Wisdom Woman, Wisdom Worldview and, finally, Wisdom and Francis.

Wisdom Literature

What exactly is the Wisdom Literature of the Old Testament? In the Christian Old Testament, the Wisdom Literature is found in the middle, with the Historical Books on one side and the Prophets on the other.[1] The books included are, in order, Job, Psalms, Proverbs, Ecclesiastes (also known as Qoheleth), Song of Songs, The Book of Wisdom (a.k.a. Wisdom of Solomon), and The Book of Sirach (a.k.a. Ecclesiasticus). Psalms and Song of Songs have a unique character. Their relationship to the Wisdom Literature is variously assessed.[2] The "big three" only—Proverbs, Job and Ecclesiastes—are found in Jewish and Protestant Bibles.

The Wisdom Literature has several features that set it apart from the rest and give it a unique character. It seldom speaks of the big, dramatic experiences of Israel (e.g., Exodus or Covenant), but rather has a very down-to-earth feel. It deals with the everyday, the regular, the normal and the mundane. Wisdom depends on and speaks from experience. It is in the everyday happenings of our lives and in our reflections on them—expressed often as proverbs—that we find wisdom and teaching from God.

The purpose of this part of the biblical tradition can be summed up in Proverbs 1:2: "for learning about wisdom and instruction." Wisdom (*hokmah*) is basically the ability to do a good job in whatever area, but it expands to include the ability to live in harmony with the world and with other people. It includes such virtues as intelligence, shrewdness, common sense and sound judgment. Instruction (*musar*) involves the ability to learn lessons from life: "Then I saw and considered it; I looked and received instruction" (Prov 24:32). The result of such instruction is the ability to behave well in differing situations. Both wisdom and instruction are not just intellectual qualities, but are manifested in behavior. Persons are only as wise as they act.[3]

In the last thirty years or so, biblical studies have seen quite a revival of interest in Wisdom Literature. Before then, with a few exceptions, it suffered from either benign neglect or outright hostility.[4] Its positive contribution to the overall theology of the Old Testament, its importance as background to the New Testament and its relevance to issues of contemporary concern have all contributed to this revival.

Wisdom Quotations

Did the Wisdom Literature have an influence on St. Francis? We can begin by asking if he quotes from that literature in his writings. There are, in fact, surprisingly few references to be found. Kajetan Esser, in his critical edition of the writings of Francis, identifies only six.[5] Robert J. Karris, in his study of the *Admonitions*,[6] has sniffed out two more, for a total of eight. We will begin by simply listing them:[7]

1. In fact, there are many religious who, under the pretext of seeing things better than those which the prelate commands, look back and **return to the vomit** of their own will (Adm 3:10) [13]. Like a dog that **returns to its vomit**, is a fool who reverts to his folly (Prov 26:11).

2. Blessed is the servant who . . . is **not quick to speak**, but who is wisely cautious about what he says and how he responds (Adm 21:1) [135].
    Do you see someone who is **hasty in speech**? There is more hope for a fool than for anyone like that (Prov 29:20).

3, If we find coins anywhere, let us pay no more attention to them than to the dust we trample underfoot, for **vanity of vanities and all is vanity** (ER 8:6) [70].
    Vanity of vanities, says the Teacher, **vanity of vanities! All is vanity** (Eccl 1:2).

4. The wiser and more powerful they may have been in this world, the greater will be the punishment they will endure in hell (LR 5) [58].
    For the lowliest may be pardoned in mercy, but the mighty will be mightily tested (WisSol 6:6). (Agreement in sense.)

5. Behold, each day he humbles himself as when he came **from the royal throne** into the Virgin's womb (Adm 1:16) [129].
    And night in its swift course was now half gone, your all powerful word leaped from heaven, **from the royal throne** into the midst of the land. . . (WisSol 18:15).

6-7. Blessed is that religious who does not have **delight and happiness** except in the most holy words and deeds of the Lord, and, with these, leads people to the love of God with **gladness and joy** (Adm 20:1-2) [135].
    The fear of the Lord delights the heart, and gives **happiness and joy** and long life (Sir 1:12).
    Religiousness (i.e., fear of the Lord) will guard and justify the heart and will give [it] **delight and joy**[8] (Sir 1:18).

8. We must also fast and **abstain from** vices and **sins** and from an excess of food and drink and be Catholics (2LtF 32) [47].
    The one intelligent and wise in heart will **abstain from sins,** and in works of justice, he will have success[9] (Sir 3:32).

Thus, we have three from Sirach, two from Proverbs and Wisdom of Solomon, and one from Ecclesiastes.
    We can make several brief observations:

1. Francis's references are few and deal with behavior of a fairly general type.

2. Francis probably drew these from two main sources: the liturgy and the monastic spiritual tradition of his day. The reference to God's Word leaping from his royal throne (#5, from *Admonition* 1) was a familiar reading from the midnight Mass of Christmas. The references in #1 (*Admonition* 3), to a dog returning to its vomit, and in #2, 6 and 7 (*Admonitions* 20, 21) to proper use of speech, seem to have come to Francis "prepackaged in the monastic tradition."[10] We may further note that the

issue of proper speech, reflecting the oral culture of the Bible, is a very important topic in the biblical Wisdom Literature.[11]

3. Noticeably missing from Francis's quotations are the books of Song of Songs and Job. Songs of Songs was extremely important and common in the spiritual and mystical tradition of the Middle Ages.[12] Its absence is curious, and one might ask if there might be any particular reason for this. Job is largely lamentation and challenges to God based on Job's experience of God's absence. Francis is familiar with the lamentation psalms and cites them above all in his *Office of the Passion.* Interestingly, though, he omits cries of pain because of God's absence as well as the "cursing prayers" against enemies. Francis's spirituality was not one of lamentation, but of praise. We will return to this below.

4. There is something else absent from Francis's quotations, and this leads us into our next topic.

Wisdom Woman

One of the most interesting and exciting aspects of the Wisdom Literature is the figure of Lady Wisdom or the Wisdom Woman, who appears in a number of key texts (cf. esp. Prov 1:20-33; 8; Job 28; Sirach 24, Wisdom of Solomon 6-9) and develops over several centuries. Wisdom is with God and has a divine origin (e.g., Prov 8:22; Sir 24:3, 9); she is active with God in creating the universe (Prov 8:22-29; Sir 1:4; WisSol 9:9) and has a particular mission toward human beings. She calls to us in and through the world (Prov 1, 8, 9) and promises life, prosperity and every blessing to those who embrace her (Prov 1:32; 3:13-18). In later texts, she is identified with the Torah, the Law of Moses (Sir 24:23), and is recognized as at work in Israel's history (Sir 44-50; WisSol 10:1-21). While there is some difference of opinion, most scholars see in the Wisdom Woman a personification of God's wisdom and a form of God's presence in and through the world.[13]

This theme is an important one today in identifying feminine images of God in the Old Testament and provides important background for understanding Jesus in the New.[14] It would be very nice to find some echoes of this in the writings and vision of St. Francis. Unfortunately, none of the texts associated with this figure appears in his writings. I think it is worth noting this, because at times the temptation to look for (and to find?) important contemporary issues back in our founding sources can be very strong. Francis does speak of Jesus as the Wisdom of God, but does not seem to derive it from these texts.[15] We have to recognize and respect the fact that Francis of Assisi was a medieval man.

Wisdom Worldview

Looking at individual texts does not take us too far in our search for Wisdom influence on St. Francis. A look at the Wisdom worldview provides a more productive approach.

"Wisdom thinks resolutely within the framework of a theology of creation."[16] When this was first proposed over forty years ago, it was a bit of a breakthrough; but it has since become a truism of Wisdom study. In fact, a whole book has been devoted to looking at every reference to creation in the Wisdom books.[17]

When we speak of "creation," what exactly are we speaking of? Creation is not the same as "nature." Neither is it a properly scientific or philosophical term. Creation is a thoroughly religious concept. To understand everything that exists at its deepest level, it must be seen in relationship to God. And this is a statement not only about beginnings but is true at every single moment of time. Creation always implies a Creator; the two go together and mutually imply each other. We will look first at God as Creator in Wisdom, then at what it is that God has made.

God as Creator

Whenever we speak of God, we are using some kind of metaphor or image drawn from and based in our everyday experience. The psalmist exclaims: "O Lord, how manifold are your works! In wisdom you have made them all!" (Ps 104:24). In response to Job's pleas, God describes the creation process as a builder following a blueprint: "Where were you when I laid the foundation of the earth?" (Job 38:4-11). In Proverbs we read: "The Lord by wisdom founded the earth" (Prov 3:19). What is the image being invoked here? As we noted above, the basic meaning of "wisdom" (*hokmah*) is "skill, the ability to do a good job." God is presented as a skilled craftsman, an artisan who has fashioned a universe.[18] It is this "wisdom of God" which is personified as the Wisdom Woman. As important a theme as this is, however, we will not trace its development here.[19]

God is a skilled craftsman or carpenter and has done a good job. Sirach bursts into praise: "All the works of the Lord are very good" (Sir 39:16). In this he is echoing the refrain of Genesis 1: "God saw that it was good . . . it was very good" (Gen 1:4, 10, 12, 18, 21, 25, 31). Some scholars have argued, and I would be one of them, that a better translation of "good" here would be "beautiful."[20] All the works of the Lord are very beautiful! God's wisdom and skill are reflected in "the works of his hands."

The Creation as God's Work—God's House

If God as craftsman has made a beautiful "something," what is the "thing" that God has made? When we talk about God's work, we use images and metaphors, but what about the fruit of God's work? Does Scripture provide any images by which we can understand the world?[21] In fact, there are several; but here, in the context of the Wisdom Literature, we can note two that, in fact, are closely related.

First, the world is God's house. We read in Proverbs 24:34: "By **wisdom** a house is **built**, and by **understanding** it is **established,** by **knowledge** the rooms are filled with all precious and pleasant riches." This is exactly the same language used earlier in the book to speak of God's creating: "The Lord by **wisdom** founded the earth; by **understanding** he **established** the heavens, by his **knowledge** the deeps broke open and the clouds drop down the dew" (Prov 3:19-20). In the great hymn of Proverbs 8, God's wisdom in creating is personified as the Wisdom Woman (Prov. 8:22-31), and immediately after, in Proverbs 9:1, we read a summary statement, "Wisdom has built her house, she has hewn her seven pillars" (see also 14:1). "Her pillars suggest those used to support the roof of a large building . . . or the columns founded upon the earth to hold up the cosmic sky."[22] In Proverbs 8:31, we read that Wisdom was "rejoicing in his inhabited world and delighting in the human race." And in Proverbs 9:2-6, Lady Wisdom sends out her invitation to come for a meal. William P. Brown describes this as "the World as Wisdom's playhouse."[23]

Since the Lord created/built the house, the universe, with wisdom and understanding, how are we humans supposed to live in this house? The psalmist admonishes us: "Unless the Lord builds the house, those who build it labor in vain" (Ps 127:1). We are urged to seek and to live with wisdom and understanding. "Happy are those who find **wisdom,** and those who get **understanding**" (Prov 3:13). When we do this, we put ourselves in line with God's creative power and activity. We are called to be and become co-creators, co-builders with God. God's wisdom/skill, manifested in the world (the "God-built house"), is the model of all "skill in living," of all human wisdom.

Creation as God's Work—God's Temple

Second, a different but closely related image comes into play. The world is "God's house." But when the phrase "house of God" or "house of the Lord" is used in the Old Testament, it most often refers to a rather specific house—the house of the Lord par excellence, the temple in Jerusalem (cf., 2 Sam 7:13; 1 Kgs 4:5). The ancient temple had a double significance. It was the place where the presence of God was most focused, most intense, and it was the place where human worship of God was expressed. Ancient temples did have cosmic symbolism. They were the places where creation and humanity were most "in order"; each temple was a microcosm, a "small-universe."[24] When construction of the temple in Jerusalem begins, we are told that Hiram of Tyre, the chief contractor as it were, was full of **wisdom** (skill), **understanding** and **knowledge** (1 Kgs 7:13)—the same attributes manifested by God in creating the cosmos (Prov 3:19-20).[25]

If the world is God's house, then it is also, in some sense, God's temple. World-building and temple-building go together. They are, as it were, a big picture and a small picture of the same thing.[26] A good analogy is offered by modern technology! Think of the "minimize" button on the computer window. When you click on it, the "big picture" is reduced to a "little picture" on the tool bar; when you click on that, the "big picture" reemerges. The temple is the little picture; all of creation is the big one. The temple is a microcosm; the universe is a macro-temple. In the light of this, we can appreciate Psalm 148: "Praise the Lord from the heavens. . . .Praise the Lord from the earth," and then all of creation is called on to offer praise: sun and moon, stars, waters above the heavens, sea creatures, fire and hail, snow and frost, wind, mountains, hills, trees, animals wild and tame, people, high and low, young and old, men and women together. The cosmic temple is filled with the full-voiced choir of praise. (See also the song of the three young men in Daniel 3:52-90.) Thus house-building, temple-building and cosmos-building are all held together.[27]

A Christian Temple/House of God

So far we have restricted our attention to the Wisdom texts of the Old Testament, but what about Christian texts? The temple in Jerusalem was destroyed by the Romans in 70 A.D. and has never been rebuilt. Further, Jesus told the Samaritan woman by the well: "The hour is coming when you will worship the Father neither on this mountain nor in

Jerusalem" (John 4:21). We do have church buildings and cathedrals. Do these function for us now as surrogate temples?

The fact is, we do have a temple, and it has all of the meaning that we have discussed so far. This is an important theme in the Gospel of John. We can point briefly to two indications:

1) In the prologue, John tells us that the Word, present with God from all eternity, the Word through and with whom all was created, "became flesh and lived among us [literally 'pitched his tent among us'], and we have seen his glory" (1:14). Like the Wisdom Woman, Jesus embodies the Wisdom of God. Israel's tent/tabernacle, pitched in the wilderness, was a foreshadowing of the Jerusalem temple. Tabernacle and Temple have the same symbolism. And, just as the "glory of God," the sign of God's special presence, covered the tabernacle and the temple (Ex 40:34; 1 Kgs 8:10-11), so it is present in Jesus.

2) To make it even more explicit, in chapter two of John's Gospel, after Jesus cleanses the temple, the Jews are upset and ask: "What sign can you show us for doing this?" Jesus answers them: "Destroy this temple, and in three days I will raise it up." When they misunderstand (a common phenomenon in John's gospel), the evangelist tells us: "He was speaking of the temple of his body" (John 2:18-22).

We move from creation to temple—the temple that is the flesh of the Word. The incarnate Jesus embodies in himself the meaning and reality of the temple—the place where the presence of God is most concentrated, and the place where the full worship of creatures is rendered to God. Some Jewish writers roughly contemporary with the writing of the New Testament show that they realize the cosmic symbolism of the temple. Philo and Josephus "interpret the tabernacle as a symbol of the cosmos and occasionally apply a similar interpretation to the Jerusalem temple."[28] In the light of this, we can apply what we said above, namely, that the temple is a microcosm, and the cosmos is a macro-temple. In the Christian understanding, the body of Christ is a microcosm, and the cosmos is a macro-body of Christ. The universe, then, is "the body of Christ." Click on the universe and it is "reduced" to the body of Christ; click on the body of Christ, it enlarges to the universe. The incarnate Jesus embodies both the wisdom of God through and with whom the universe was created and the "good/beautiful" work of God, the cosmos-temple-house.

In light of the above, we might ask: "Where are we, in fact, living?" Whether we are aware of it or not, whether we like it or not, whether we do it well or badly, we are all immersed in "the body of the Word," which is the cosmos. St. Bonaventure develops this in his teaching that God's revelation comes to us in two books—the Book of Scripture and the Book of Creation—and both of these are read with a similar hermeneutics: there is a surface or literal meaning and a deeper or spiritual meaning.[29]

Wisdom and St. Francis

We can now conclude with some comments on St. Francis and Wisdom. While he does not draw on many Wisdom texts in his writings, I think we can safely say that he lived in and out of a Wisdom worldview. It might be closer to say that he reveled in it.

First, Francis is overwhelmed by the goodness of the gifts of God. His favorite adjective for God is good, and he cannot say it often enough. On the *chartula* given to Brother Leo, Francis wrote his praises of God: You are the good, all good, the highest good (PrsG 3), and in his prayer inspired by the Our Father: "You Lord, are Supreme Good, the Eternal Good, from Whom all good comes, without Whom there is no good" (PrOF 2). And in keeping with Genesis 1, Francis affirms, twice in the same breath, that God is beauty (PrsG 4-5).

Second, Francis's favorite response to the goodness of God is praise. In the Bible, the most characteristic response to the blessings of creation is praise. Praise calls out to others and focuses on the Giver and the Gift.[30] "Praise the Lord . . . because . . . the Lord has been good to me!" Francis experienced his whole life and everything in it as good gifts of the good God. His response was praise. Even when faced with death, he praised God for Sister Death (CtC 12). This may point to a deeper reason why we do not find any quotations from the lamentations of Job. Though he certainly knew pain and suffering in his life, Francis was just not a lamenting person.

Third, while Francis's association with nature is certainly well known, if not the best known aspect of him, we can see that Francis is not a saint of nature at all. He is a saint of creation. For Francis, creation and Creator go together. He saw in and through creatures, the hand of their Creator God.

Fourth, Francis's best known composition is certainly the *Canticle of the Creatures*, written shortly before his death. It reflects in a poetic way, Francis's whole relationship with creation. And it is a prayer of praise. The expression "Praised be" (Italian, *laudato*) occurs nine times in the poem. There is another word that occurs ten times. It is the Italian word "*per.*" This one little word is difficult because there are three possible translations: 1) it can mean "for" or "because of," expressing an attitude of thanksgiving; 2) it can mean "by," expressing a sense of instrumentality; or 3) it could mean "through," expressing a deeper sense of seeing God's presence in and through creatures.[31] Each of these can find support in other writings of Francis as well as in the early sources about him. Each expresses something beautiful, worthy and true. All are at home in the thought of Francis. We do not have one word in English that captures all of these nuances, so we have to make a choice; but we should also keep all the meanings in mind.

Perhaps we can go a bit deeper.

- If Francis saw all of creation as God's HOUSE,[32] then perhaps he saw us, everyone and everything in creation as members of one family, children of the same God, and brothers and sisters of each other. He called all creatures brother and sister, and he praised God **FOR** the good gifts which this family was to him.

- If Francis saw all of creation as God's TEMPLE, as the place where God's presence could be experienced and where we could respond in reverent worship, then perhaps he might call on all of his family to join him in his prayer so that God might be praised **BY** the whole chorus, just as we saw in Psalm 148.

- If Francis saw all of creation as mediating the BODY of Christ to him, then he might praise God **THROUGH** all creatures.[33]

I am not suggesting that Francis arrived at this through meditating on the Wisdom Literature of the Bible. But I do believe that he lived and expressed, on a deeply personal level and in a deeply personal way, the worldview of the Wisdom Literature. And his example remains a challenge for us who try in our own ways to follow him.

- If we really believed that the world is God's house and we, all people and all creatures, are one family . . .
- If we really believed that the world is God's temple, the place where God is present and where we can respond in praise . . .
- If we really believed that the whole world and all that is in it is truly part of the body of Christ . . .

then what would our behavior look like? The call of wisdom is addressed to us today:

Happy are those who find wisdom, and those
who get understanding.
She is a tree of life to those who lay hold of her (Prov 3:12).

Endnotes

[1]In Jewish bibles, the Wisdom Literature is found in the third part, called the Writings (*Ketubim*).

[2]For introductory remarks in regard to Psalms and Song of Songs in the context of the Wisdom Literature, see Roland E. Murphy, *The Tree of Life: An Exploration of the Wisdom Literature*, 3rd ed. (Grand Rapids, MI: Wm. B. Eerdmans, 2002), 103-104, 106-107. For the most part, we will not include these in our discussion.

[3]M. Saebo, *"hkm,* to be wise," *Theological Dictionary of the Old Testament*, vol. 1, ed. E. Jenni and C. Westermann (Peabody, MA: Hendrickson, 1997): 418-24; *"ysr,* to chastise," vol. 2:548-51.

[4]For example, it was considered a "foreign body" that Israel swallowed down but never quite managed to digest (H. D. Preuss); see Murphy, *Tree of Life*, 121-26.

[5]Kajetan Esser, O.F.M., *Opuscula Sancti Patris Francisci Assisiensis*, Bibliotheca Franciscana Ascetica Medii Aevi, Tom. XII (Grottaferrata [Rome], Collegii S. Bonaventurae ad Claras Aquas, 1978), 334.

[6]Robert J. Karris, OFM, *The Admonitions of St. Francis: Sources and Meanings* (St. Bonaventure, NY: The Franciscan Institute, 1999), 281-85.

[7]The numbers in square brackets indicate the page where the quotation from Francis's writings can be found in *Francis of Assisi: Early Documents*, vol. 1: *The Saint*, ed. R. Armstrong, W. Hellmann, W. Short (New York: New City Press, 1999).

[8]These two (#6 and #7) were added by Karris, *Admonitions*, 202-203.

[9]This is found in the Latin Vulgate, the text familiar in the Middle Ages. This quotation does not appear in more recent translations based on contemporary text-critical work.

[10]Karris, *Admonitions*, 69; see also 201, 207-208, 278.

[11]For a beginning, see Murphy, *Tree of Life*, 22, 31, n. 21; also his "Excursus on Speech," in *Proverbs*, Word Biblical Commentary 22 (Nashville, TN: Thomas Nelson Publishers, 1998), 258-60.

[12]Richard A. Norris, ed., *The Song of Songs: Interpreted by the Early Church and Medieval Commentators*, The Church's Bible Series 1 (Grand Rapids, MI: Wm. B. Eerdmans, 2003).

[13]For a good introduction to this important issue and the literature associated with it, see Murphy, *Tree of Life,* 133-49, 227-29, 278-81. See also Kathleen O'Connor, "Wisdom Literature and Experience of the Divine," in *Biblical Theology: Problems and Perspectives* (Nashville, TN: Abingdon, 1995), 183-95.

[14]See Elizabeth A. Johnson, "Jesus, the Wisdom of God: A Biblical Basis for Non-Androcentric Christology," *Ephemerides Theologicae Lovanienses* 61 (1985): 261-94 and her later incorporation of this in *She Who Is: The Mystery of God in Feminist Theological Discourse* (New York: Crossroads, 1992).

[15]See Norbert Nguyen-Van-Khanh, *The Teacher of His Heart: Jesus Christ in the Thought and Writings of St. Francis* (St. Bonaventure, NY: Franciscan Institute Press, 1994), 121-23.

[16]Walter Zimmerli, "The Place and the Limit of Wisdom in the Framework of the Old Testament Theology," *Studies in Ancient Israelite Wisdom,* ed. James Crenshaw (New York: KTAV Publishing House, 1976), 316. Zimmerli's article first appeared in 1964 when biblical studies were focused almost exclusively on "salvation-history" concerns.

[17]Leo G. Perdue, *Wisdom and Creation: The Theology of the Wisdom Literature* (Nashville, TN: Abingdon, 1994).

[18]See my "Images of God in the Wisdom Literature," *The Bible Today* 38 (2000): 223-27. Other images occur in Scripture as well, e.g., a commander giving orders (creation by word, e.g. Ps 33:6, 9) and a mighty warrior defeating chaos (Ps. 74:12-17). On these and others, see Walter Brueggemann, *Theology of the Old Testament: Testimony, Dispute, Advocacy* (Minneapolis, MN: Fortress Press, 1997), 145-64.

[19]See footnote 14 above.

[20]See Claus Westermann, *Genesis 1-11* (Minneapolis, MN: Augsburg Press, 1984), 166; see also 113: "A craftsman has completed a work, he looks at it and finds that it is a success. . . ."

[21]We can note here that biblical Hebrew does not have a word that means "universe." Instead, it uses expressions like "the heavens and the earth" or "all/the totality."

[22]Perdue, *Wisdom and Creation*, 95. On pillared houses in ancient Israel, see Philip J. King and Lawrence E. Stager, *Life in Biblical Israel,* Library of Ancient Israel (Louisville, KY: Westminster John Knox Press, 2001), 28-35.

[23]William P. Brown, *The Ethos of the Cosmos: The Genesis of Moral Imagination in the Bible* (Grand Rapids, MI: Wm. B.Eerdmans, 1999), 271-316.

[24]For beginning discussion, see Jon D. Levenson, "The Temple and the World," *Journal of Religion* 64 (1984): 275-98; see also his *Creation and the Persistence of Evil: The Jewish Drama of Divine Omnipotence* (San Francisco, CA: Harper and Row, 1988), 78-99.

[25]There are those who see temple symbolism in Proverbs 9 as well. See Perdue, *Wisdom and Creation*, 95-97; William P. Brown, *Character in Crisis: A Fresh Approach to the Wisdom Literature of the Old Testament* (Grand Rapids, MI: Wm. B.Eerdmans, 1996), 40.

[26]There is considerable study of the connection between the creation account of Genesis 1 and the building of the tabernacle (temple) in the wilderness in Exodus 25-40. See among others, Brown, *Ethos of the Cosmos*, 73-89; Samuel E. Ballentine, *The Torah's Vision of Worship, Overtures to Biblical Theology* (Minneapolis, MN: Fortress, 1999), 136-42; Terence E. Fretheim, *Exodus, Interpretation Commentary* (Louisville, KY: John Knox Publishing, 1991), 264-78.

[27]See the brief but pertinent remarks of Raymond C. Van Leeuwen on Proverbs 9 in "The Book of Proverbs," *New Interpreter's Bible* 5 (Nashville, TN: Abingdon, 1997) 101-102. The Bible is well aware that there is folly in the house and sin and uncleanness in the temple; the images of creation it presents represent God's ultimate purposes and stand in judgment on any here and now situation.

[28]Craig R. Koester, *The Dwelling of God: The Tabernacle in the Old Testament, Intertestamental Jewish Literature, and the New Testament,* CBQMS 22 (Washington, DC: The Catholic Biblical Association, 1989), 59-63. He discusses John's gospel on pp. 100-15. For a full development of this theme, see Mary L. Coloe, *God Dwells With Us: Temple Symbolism in the Fourth Gospel* (Collegeville, MN: Liturgical Press, 2001).

[29]See Zachary Hayes, O.F.M., "Bonaventure: Mystery of the Triune God," in *The History of Franciscan Theology,* ed. Kenan B. Osborne, O.F.M. (St. Bonaventure, NY: The Franciscan Institute, 1994), 72-79 and, more popularly, Ilia Delio, O.S.F., *Simply Bonaventure: An Introduction to His Life, Thought and Writings* (New York: New City Press, 2001), 54-66.

[30]For a popular introduction to the meaning of praise in the Bible, see my "The Book of Psalms: Prayers for Everyday Living, " *St. Anthony Messenger* 112.8 (January, 2005): 13-16.

[31]See footnote "a" on page 114 of FAED, I. This translation chooses "through."

[32]We recall that at the beginning of Francis's conversion, Jesus spoke to him from the San Damiano cross: "Francis, go repair my house. . . ." FAED II, 76 [L3C 13], 249 [2C 10], 536 [LMj 2:1].

[33]This is unpacked theologically by St. Bonaventure in his theology of exemplarism. See the references in footnote 29 above.

Authors

Vincent Cushing, O.F.M., of Holy Name Province, was president of Washington Theological Union from 1975 to 1999. He has since been honored as *President Emeritus* by the Union's Board of Trustees. He has completed terms on the board of the National Catholic Education Association Executive Committee, on the Formation Committee of the Conference of Major Superiors of Men, as well as on the Steering Committee of the Bishops' Committee on Priestly Formation. In addition, he has been a member of the Executive Committee of the Association of Theological Schools, serving as its president from 1982 to 1984.

Robert J. Karris, O.F.M., Th.D. in New Testament Studies, is now in his eighth year as a member of the research faculty at the Franciscan Institute, St. Bonaventure University, and has been dedicating his research to St. Bonaventure's biblical commentaries. Having published the three volumes of annotated translations of Bonaventure's *Commentary on the Gospel of Luke* and co-published an annotated translation of Bonaventure's *Commentary on Ecclesiastes*, he is now preparing an annotated translation of Bonaventure's *Commentary on John's Gospel.* Between times he publishes New Testament books such as *Eating Your Way through Luke's Gospel* (Liturgical Press, 2006). He is a member of Sacred Heart Province.

Michael D. Guinan, O.F.M., has been a friar of the Saint Barbara Province (California) since 1959. He completed his doctoral studies in Semitic Languages and Literatures at the Catholic University of America, Washington, DC. He has taught Old Testament and Semitics at the Franciscan School of Theology, Berkeley, since 1972. In addition, he taught in the summer theology program at St. Bonaventure University, 1972-1982. From 1984-1997, he taught during the summers at Our Lady of the Angels Seminary (and then the Intercommunity Theological Consortium) in Metro Manila, Philippines. He contributed to the *New Jerome Biblical Commentary* (Book of Lamentations), the *Collegeville Bible Commentary* (Book of Job) and the *Message of Biblical Spirituality* series (The Pentateuch). He has done a number of articles for *St. Anthony Messenger* and for the *Catholic Update* series.

Dominic V. Monti, O.F.M., is currently serving as Vice-Provincial of Holy Name Province, New York. He received his Ph.D. at the University of Chicago, where he studied under Bernard McGinn. He was a member of the Theology Department at St. Bonaventure University from 2002 to 2005 and served as interim President of the University for one year. He taught at Washington Theological Union from 1979 to 2002 in the Department of Ecclesiastical History and was chair of the department. In 1994, he contributed translations of Bonaventure's *Writings Concerning the Franciscan Order,* Bonaventure Texts in Translation Series, Vol. V (St. Bonaventure, NY: The Franciscan Institute, 1994). He made significant contributions to *Francis of Assisi: Early Documents* (New York: New City Press, 1999-2001) and has recently completed a new translation of Bonaventure's *Breviloquium* (Franciscan Institute Publications, 2005).

James P. Scullion, O.F.M., is a Franciscan Friar of Holy Name Province. Since 1989 he has been Assistant Professor of Sacred Scripture at the Washington Theological Union. He has served at the Union as Vice-President for Academic Affairs and Academic Dean (2000-2002) and has been involved in the formation program for his Province as Assistant Director of Post-Novitiate Formation and Vicar (1991-1999, 2002-2004). Prior to his studies and teaching he was an Associate Pastor at St. Bonaventure Parish, Paterson, NJ (1979-81). He has served on the editorial board of *New Theology Review* and currently is a scripture consultant and writer for *Share the Word.* He has published articles on various New Testament topics as well as on the use of Information Technology in the classroom. He contributed a chapter, "Creation-Incarnation: God's Affirmation of Human Worth," in *Made in God's Image: The Catholic Vision of Human Dignity* (Paulist Press, 1999).